THE LADY IN THE LAKE

THE LADY IN THE LAKE

JEREMY CRADDOCK

MIRROR BOOKS

MIRROR BOOKS

© Jeremy Craddock

1

Published in Great Britain and Ireland in 2024 by
Mirror Books, a Reach PLC business.

www.mirrorbooks.co.uk
@TheMirrorBooks

Print ISBN 9781915306685
eBook ISBN 9781915306692

Cover Design: Chris Collins
Editor: Christine Costello

Printed and bound in Great Britain by
CPI Group (UK) Ltd, Croydon, CR0 4YY

MIX
Paper | Supporting
responsible forestry
FSC® C171272

To Louise, Emily and Matthew

Contents

CONTENTS

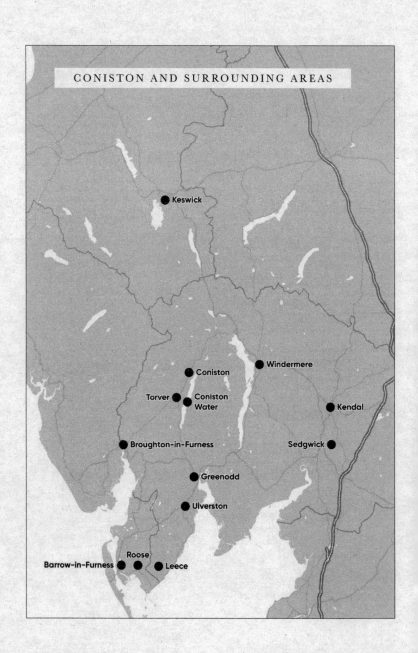

CONISTON AND SURROUNDING AREAS

Keswick

Windermere

Coniston

Torver   Coniston
         Water

Kendal

Broughton-in-Furness

Sedgwick

Greenodd

Ulverston

Roose

Barrow-in-Furness   Leece

Prologue

The Lady in the Lake was the strangest, most intriguing English murder case of the late 20th century. It was a rare mystery that unfolded across five decades, bleeding into the new millennium. It is a narrative woven with lies and heartbreak for a divided family, a story of dogged detective work, of reporters feeding a terrible tale to an electrified public.

This book has been a long time coming, much longer than it took to write. The case has been in my thoughts for a quarter of a century. It was a murder close to where I grew up. I was seven and living in the Lake District not so far from Carol Park when she went missing in the summer of 1976. My parents were about the same age as Carol and her husband Gordon. On the face of it the Park family was not so different from my own.

When her body was found in Coniston Water in 1997, I was 28 and a reporter for the local newspaper. When the case was laid to rest in 2020 I was a 51-year-old author. This book is the first to tell the complete, tragic story. Its seeds lay in my evolution from journalist to author.

I had always wanted to be a writer. Over the years I attempted novels and plays, keeping my creative writing separate from my journalism. Then one day I decided to synthesise the two: true stories told like fiction. All I needed was a story. The search led me to my first book, *The Jigsaw Murders*. That was a haunting case, a double murder my Dad told me about, now lost in the mists of time. The gruesome crimes of Dr Buck Ruxton in Lancaster in 1935 had been a newspaper sensation. Ruxton murdered his wife and children's nanny, cut up their bodies and disposed of the remains in a Scottish ravine. The pioneering investigation by police and forensic scientists resulted in new techniques still in use today.

True crime wasn't a genre I was especially drawn to but this was such a strong story and I knew I could tell it more vividly than it had been told before. I had read a number of seminal true crime books and for that I have my late mother to thank. She had a deep interest in the subject. In another life she might have been a criminologist. When I was growing up I remember her reading *Helter Skelter* about Charles Manson, *Beyond Belief*, Emlyn Williams's account of the Moors Murders, and Gordon Burn's *Somebody's Husband, Somebody's Son*, about Yorkshire Ripper Peter Sutcliffe. Mum would hide these publications from my eyes. Needless to say, I found them, riffled the pages and scared myself witless.

Where did Mum's interest spring from? Two events may hold the answer.

Her father was a prison officer for a number of years at Risley Prison near Warrington. In 1966 when Moors Murderers Ian Brady and Myra Hindley were on remand, he was one of the guards who escorted Brady to the trial at Chester Assizes. Mum said my grandfather would never talk about the harrowing tape played in court of the torture of Lesley Ann Downey.

The second event was when I was 12. My parents owned a caravan on the edge of Morecambe Bay. We spent weekends and our summer holidays there. Our van sat in woodland above a pretty shingle beach called White Creek. One of the neighbouring caravans belonged to the family of Peter Sutcliffe, who had spent holidays there as a youth. When he was convicted in 1981, people on the site began referring to the 'Ripper's van'. I still remember Mum's keen interest in newspaper coverage of the trial.

After *The Jigsaw Murders* was published I was invited to talk at the international CrimeCon festival in London and the book was nominated for the Crime Writers' Association Gold Dagger for Non Fiction.

I was amazed by the intense interest in the true crime genre. Why were people so hooked on real murders? As part of a newspaper feature I was writing, I spoke to two psychologists about the phenomenon. They told me our enduring fascination with crime is hard-wired, linked to our survival instinct. We try to imagine how we'd cope in such awful circumstances while taking comfort from the knowledge that it happened to somebody else.

In January 2023 I was in the Lake District to give a talk at Waterstones bookshop in Kendal. During questions somebody asked about the stories I'd covered as a reporter. I found myself talking about the Lady in the Lake case. The audience sat up. Most had heard of it, many remembered its tragic reverberations.

Afterwards, as I signed books, a man in his seventies approached the table and told me he had been a keen diver in his younger days and had explored Coniston Water, the lake at the heart of the case.

"It's very dark in there," he said, "you can barely see in front of you."

I winced. I've always feared deep, dark water.

"I would read a book about that case," he said. I detected a note of encouragement in his voice.

At the heart of the story was a young mother who went missing in the 1970s. The day after my visit to Kendal, the biggest news story in the UK was the disappearance of another young mother, Nicola Bulley, in rural Lancashire, who was suspected of having fallen into a river and drowned. Yet the intense news and social media coverage of Nicola's 2023 disappearance stood in stark contrast to the way the case of a missing woman had been reported by the press 50 years earlier. That is to say, the 1976 Carol Park case hardly merited a mention at the time.

How times had changed, I thought. Even the way journalists worked when I began in the 1990s now seemed antiquated. Research then meant a trip to the library, not a click of Google. Today I teach journalism at Manchester Metropolitan University and when I stand in the lecture theatre describing these changes I wonder whether my students think I'm joking.

Go to the library?!

The trip to Kendal, my hometown, had been fruitful. It had underlined what had happened in the years since I first wrote about the Lady in the Lake case in 1997 and the shifts in my own life circumstances across 25 years. Both my parents had died recently and earlier in the day I had laid flowers on their grave. I'd visited my childhood home and found it hard to accept it wasn't Mum and Dad but a stranger living there now.

I started to think about the family at the heart of the Coniston Water case and what had happened to them since.

Back home in Cheshire, I popped down the loft ladder and climbed into the space under the eaves. I was looking for my old newspaper cuttings, keen to see if I still had my original reports from 1997. I had stopped keeping cuttings after a while. I wrote so much day in day out, stories whose relevance quickly expired, that the novelty wore off. I found my cuttings files, carried them down the ladder and began flicking through the pages. My eye ran swiftly over the crisp, discoloured headlines but there was nothing about the case. It didn't surprise me: much of the newspaper's work on big stories was collaborative. Often no byline was attributed as the words had passed through many hands by the time they were printed.

But I had been there in 1997, to bear witness to the start of this tragic case. Suddenly I knew I wanted to explore what had happened, to find out whether justice had been served. I knew I wanted to write this book.

Every story begins with a pledge: the storyteller promises the reader a tale worth telling. A story without an ending is no story at all. In 1997, like everyone else, I had no sense of an ending, nor did I know how its effect would stay with me all these years. Now it is time to tell the story to its conclusion. To fulfil the pledge.

This is the story of the Lady in the Lake murder case. It is also the story of a reporter, just one of many, many reporters who were there.

"Sleep the sleep that knows not breaking."

— Sir Walter Scott, *The Lady of the Lake*

PART ONE

THE LADY
IN THE LAKE

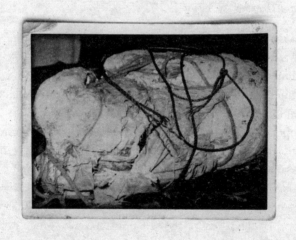

1

The Body

Cumbria. Sunday, 10 August 1997

It was warm and sunny, just after lunchtime, when the divers waded into Coniston Water. The surface of the lake was machined steel. It was as near perfect conditions as you could imagine. The three men wore black neoprene wetsuits and breathing tanks strapped to their backs. Gently, silently, they disappeared into the embrace of the lake. Coniston Water is five miles long and roughly a mile wide. It is Cumbria's third-largest lake by volume after Windermere and Ullswater, the fifth-largest by area. Peering down across the lake's western shore is the Old Man of Coniston, one of the fabled Lake District peaks; the pretty village of Coniston is a half-mile stroll to the north west. Brantwood, the home of 19th century writer and philosopher John Ruskin sits contemplatively on the eastern shore of the lake.

The divers went into the water at Bailiff Wood on the eastern edge of the lake, an area dense with woodland. This has always been a popular dive site, safe for qualified divers of all levels.

Pike, char and trout dart in and around long-forgotten detritus scattered on the lake bed, fallen from passing boats: a bath, a toilet, garden gnomes.

The lake is popular too with kayakers and canoeists and there is a mandatory 10 miles-per-hour speed limit in force for all watercraft. Yet it is for a world water speed record attempt that Coniston is anchored in the popular imagination. In January 1967, Donald Campbell was killed when his boat Bluebird turned a catastrophic cartwheel across the lake after touching 300 miles per hour.

The three divers were members of the amateur Kendal and Lakes Sub-Aqua Club. Their names were David Mason, John Walsh and David Walker. They enjoyed diving in search of interesting objects lost on the lake bed, such as old boat motors. They knew this part of Coniston well but the overfamiliarity had today prompted them to venture deeper into the cold belly of the lake. The prospect was exhilarating. It was also a little unnerving.

They set a dive depth of 25 metres and pushed on.

It is incredibly murky and dark below the surface of Coniston. Visibility can be under two metres and divers are lost without a torch. On this day, they could see up to six metres in front of them. They swam out around seven yards from the shore, going deeper and deeper to a depth of about 15 metres when they reached what looked like an underwater cliff running steeply down to a silty bank. They followed this line, down, down, until they came within metres of a ledge overhanging the deepest and darkest part of the lake. Beyond this point was uncertainty, a drop into utter blackness and the bottom of the lake 50 metres below.

The divers ventured no further as something caught their eye.

They were 16 minutes into their dive. Out of the murk they had seen something that startled them. The criss-crossing beams of their torches fell on an unexpected object lying five metres or so from the lip of the ledge. It was an eerie sight. They would later speak of a feeling of creeping apprehension. Mason made a note of their depth using his diving watch: they were roughly 24 metres below the surface. At first he thought the object might be a rock but as he swam closer he reckoned it was a bag of some sort, perhaps a sail bag. One end was tied up by a draw cord. The bag was very tightly packed and trussed up with two ropes. He wondered if there might be an old motor inside or an inflatable dinghy, something that had fallen off a passing boat overhead.

Had the object fallen several metres further into Coniston it would have disappeared into the black of the lake unlikely to ever be found. He tried to lift the bag by the ropes but it was too heavy. There was something weighing it down. The divers motioned to each other. Frustrated, they decided to leave it and complete their morning's dive.

The bag was all they could think about as they emerged from the lake. They resolved to return another day with appropriate equipment to raise it to the surface.

That evening word of the discovery spread through the dive club. Another member who lived in Kendal told his neighbour about it. "They're going to bring it ashore," he said. "You never know, there might be a body inside." The neighbour was Mike Addison. He was a journalist. The diver knew this piece of information would pique his interest.

"If there is, Mike, I'll let you know. It could be a big story."

Addison smiled. It was the sort of comment journalists heard all the time.

On Wednesday, August 13, Mason, Walsh and Walker returned to Coniston Water. They made their way back to the eerie spot, just metres from the ledge. They had brought a diver's lift bag. They carried that same feeling of apprehension.

The visibility was poor and the men swam past the package a number of times. It was about two metres from a rocky outcrop which confused them. They eventually found it again and swam down to it. They attached a D-ring using a carabiner clip to the rope around the package and then with the inflated bag swam to the surface of the lake. The bag's cable tightened and the package rose from its resting place like a sea creature emerging from a long slumber.

The men's heads broke the surface of the lake, then the lift bag. They swam to the shoreline, heading to a level sandy beach with loose stones which allowed them to wash the package ashore. They dragged it a little way on to the beach and pulled off their goggles to inspect their haul properly in daylight for the first time.

The package felt hard when prodded and it was tightly tied up. It was about four feet in length and 18 inches wide. It consisted of a stone-coloured canvas holdall with a draw cord. The divers' curiosity was overwhelming but they sensed a need to be cautious. Mason unsheathed his diver's knife. With the sharp edge he began to cut at the rope binding. Once it was severed, the bag gaped slightly and a piece of lead piping fell out of the package.

The divers looked at each other with uneasiness.

Whoever was responsible had weighted the package down with the intention of it never being found.

Apprehensively, Mason cut the outer bag by 12 inches. Inside was a green bag and, inside that, two plastic bin liners. With the tip of his knife, he drew a slit of six inches, just enough to peek inside. The contents were white and had the texture of chicken. They were looking at a shoulder blade. The contents of the package were a human body.

Detective Constable Doug Marshall was at the Railway pub in Dalton-in-Furness when the phone rang behind the bar. It was early evening and it was 27-year-old Marshall's night off. Marshall had black hair, was slim and wore glasses. He had dispensed with his work suit and was relaxing in jeans and a T-shirt. It was match night in the local pool league in which he competed. The call was for him. He was perplexed: nobody ever rang him at the pub, not even his family. He put down his cue and took the phone. It was a work colleague and there was a note of panic in his voice. Marshall and his colleague were both detectives based at Ulverston and they took it in turns to be on call in the evening. By rights, it was Marshall's colleague's turn, but he was in a dilemma. He was an amateur musician on the local pub scene. "Oh God, Doug, I'm just about to go on stage and start singing. Can you take this call for me? There's a body been found in Coniston Water."

It was a 10-minute drive from Dalton to Ulverston Police Station where Marshall switched to a police car. Then with trepidation he set off for Coniston. It dawned on him that he was at a disadvantage because he was from Penrith and didn't know the road to Coniston very well. His colleague was a local and would have known the route without reference to a map.

Marshall drove north to Spark Bridge and then had to work out the quickest route to Bailiff Wood. From the map it was clear he would circuit the eastern edge of the lake making his way north, skirting close to the water's edge on a road weaving through woodland. The deeper you go into the central Lake District the more restrictive the roads are, shrinking from fast dual carriageways and A-roads to narrow, winding country lanes with dry stone walls on either side. Meeting oncoming traffic can be tricky as you hunt for a passing place or fold your wing mirror in and pray to a greater power as you squeeze past. Tight controls on light pollution in the Lake District National Park also mean at night you are driving in almost pitch black.

Marshall reached Bailiff Wood, which was a couple of miles south of Brantwood, John Ruskin's home, and found the beach area had been cordoned off. Powerful police spotlights on poles made the scene look like a film set. He introduced himself and took stock of the situation. The divers had called the police from a phone box and just after 9.30pm two police constables arrived and had been directed by diver David Mason to the package by the lake, not far from the Bailiff Wood car park. At 10.30pm, one of the police officers had used scissors to cut the outer canvas bag to reveal the inner bin liners. A bent piece of lead pipe attached by blue twine was clearly evident. He had opened the bag enough to reveal the body. Grey climbing or sailing rope had been tied and bound to the right shoulder blade and wrapped around the body at least three times.

This had been established shortly before the arrival of Marshall, who was still dressed in jeans and T-shirt and a light jacket. The detective spoke with the diving party. Despite the shock of their find they were in good spirits. He later said the divers' caution had helped to preserve the evidence. "They were very sensible and public-spirited," he said. "They realised straight away it wasn't what they expected and they left things." A woman with the diving party handed Marshall the dive record as evidence, which he later stowed in the safe at Ulverston Police Station.

Marshall took time to inspect the grim package for himself. It appeared to be the remains of a female, dressed in a blue nightdress, in a bad state of decomposition. The head had become detached from the rest of the body. "I have quite vivid recollection of the head and the body and how things looked," Marshall recalled a quarter of a century later.

Police work at a crime scene is slow and methodical. At 11.05pm a scenes-of-crime officer photographed the body and package. Marshall awaited the arrival of senior detectives travelling down from Cumbria Police headquarters at Penrith. Detective Superintendent Ian Douglas was the SIO – senior investigating officer – and his deputy on the case would be Detective Chief Inspector Noel Kelly, who was known informally as 'Ned'. Both were experienced detectives and highly respected by their team.

Scenes-of-crime investigators finished their work and arrangements were made with a local undertaker to remove the body to the mortuary at Furness General Hospital in Barrow. Marshall recalls the process as being done with great care: "You've still got to be respectful despite the fact the body might be in a terrible condition. It's still somebody's relative."

The victim in the lake was removed at 1.55am on what was now the following day, Thursday, 14 August.

DCI Kelly briefed Marshall on what should happen next. He

told the young detective to set up an incident room at Barrow Police Station that morning in preparation for a briefing he and DS Douglas would lead. It was evident they were dealing with foul play.

Detective Constable Doug Marshall knew there wouldn't be much sleep ahead. He didn't know it but he would be involved in the case for the next quarter of a century.

2

Who Is She?

Tuesday, 12 August 1997 was my second wedding anniversary. I was on holiday with my wife, Louise, in Malta and oblivious to the events in the Lake District. As we strolled around in the sunshine there was only one news story as far as we could see. Front-page headlines on day-old British newspapers repeated the same two words: Diana, Dodi, accompanied by long-lens pictures of the Princess of Wales in a swimming costume on a yacht.

News was my trade: I was a reporter on a weekly newspaper in the Lake District, the *Westmorland Gazette*. I was 28. I had written for the paper for almost five years. It was my first job. Louise worked as a primary school teacher so our holidays were always restricted to the summer break which meant paying exorbitant prices. We usually waited as late as possible before booking, hoping for a cheap last-minute deal. It was like playing Russian roulette and we'd definitely taken a bullet with our Maltese hotel in Birzebbuga. Our room was an afterthought: a bed and a shower squeezed into an airless space. It had a single window opening onto the ventilation shaft from the hotel's kitchen from which seeped the smell of overused cooking oil.

Our stay would be memorable for all the wrong reasons. On our first day we sat around the hotel's rooftop swimming pool in the sun, smug at having it to ourselves. We realised our error later when Louise came down with sunstroke, her back bubbling with blisters. Once she was recovered we booked a tour of the island to see sights such as Valletta market and the silent city of Mdina. All went well as we rattled around in a dusty, beat-up minibus. That was until a reckless young motorist ploughed his car into the side of the bus. Everyone on board was shaken but unhurt. Miraculously the driver of the car emerged dazed but unscathed to inspect the steam rising from the crushed nose of his vehicle.

It was with a sense of relief that our plane touched down at Manchester Airport on Saturday, 16 August. We stayed overnight at my in-laws' in Cheshire and drove back to our home in Lancaster the next day. We opened the pile of mail on the mat and divested the contents of our cases into the washing machine. I would return to work the following morning.

Waiting for me would be the biggest crime story of my newspaper career.

Thursday, 14 August 1997

DC Doug Marshall was at Barrow Police Station early, only a few hours after the body had been taken to the mortuary. He had barely slept but he was riding the adrenalin. In his decade of police work he had investigated many murders. Too many.

He joined Cumbria Police as a cadet in 1986 aged 17. He was originally from Penrith, a market town in the Eden valley in the north of Cumbria. It was policy to send recruits away from their home during training so he was told he would be posted to Barrow-in-Furness, a shipbuilding town on the tip of Cumbria's south western peninsula. Cumbria has two faces. One is the exquisite landscape of spots like Coniston and Grasmere and Windermere. The other is the rugged industrial working towns of west Cumbria such as Workington, White-haven, and Barrow. Barrow's shipbuilding industry revolved around the Vickers shipyard which built warships, civilian ships and submarines and supplied armaments. Its fortunes had been precarious since the end of the Cold War. The town was the butt of jokes, cruelly seen as a dead-end hole at the end of the longest cul-de-sac in Britain. In those days, you didn't go to Barrow unless you had a reason. Before his posting, Marshall had visited only once, as a child when his father officiated at a swimming gala.

Marshall found the people of Barrow good-humoured, generous and resilient. Working out of the police station on Market Street, he pounded the beat, earning the respect of the community and impressing Cumbria Police's top brass. He was marked out as a sharp, diligent young police officer. Soon CID came calling.

He later recalled, "I was a bit reticent to start with because I was a skinny, spotty kid and CID was a tough environment. It was all typewriters, bottles of whisky, bacon sandwiches, everybody smoking. It took quite a while to get accepted."

He didn't have time to think during his early days in CID as he found himself investigating a series of double murders and isolated homicides in Barrow. It was a baptism of fire that won him the respect of the other detectives and was his rite of passage into the challenging world of CID. He was ready for his next test. "It was a thing on my appraisal: the next big job that comes along you need to be the officer in the case," he later said.

That moment had arrived and DCI Kelly had put his faith in him.

Marshall had a lot to do. He needed to set up an incident room for the murder briefing. He also had to tie up loose ends on a case he had been working on the day before the body in Coniston had been found. It involved the theft of money at a Barrow hotel. The police had laid a trap to catch the suspected thief, a member of staff. Marked notes had been planted and Marshall had to call at the home of the suspected embezzler. He recalled, "Because everybody was working on [the Coniston] case and I was setting everything up, I ended up having to go to this house in Barrow, knock on the door and say, right, I want to look in your purse. And she had all the money. I had to arrest her, take her back, interview her quickly, get her charged, get her fingerprinted and back out again so I could get onto this murder."

Back at the police station in Market Street, Marshall had the weight of responsibility on his shoulders. "I had to corral all the people who would be involved in the investigation," he said. As word of the body and murder investigation spread around the station, detectives, members of the task force and intelligence crammed into the CID office which was now in effect the incident room. This would be the nerve centre of the investigation. Marshall set up the HOLMES computer room, crucial in organising and cross-referencing information, statements and evidence that would soon begin to pour in. HOLMES was the

Home Office Large Major Enquiry System, a vital database that had been used by UK police forces since 1987. Its ability to quickly process masses of information without overlooking crucial evidence had revolutionised policing and had saved many hundreds of police man-hours. Its name was an elegant nod to the great fictional detective Sherlock Holmes.

There were around 40 police officers rammed shoulder to shoulder in the room for DS Douglas and DCI Kelly's briefing. Marshall recalled, "I've never seen so many people in that CID office. It was densely populated."

The senior detectives were succinct: a body had been found. Everything pointed to it being murder because of the manner in which the remains had been packed and weighed down. The identity of the victim was unknown. That was their primary focus: establish who the dead woman was.

Marshall had a quiet word with DCI Kelly afterwards. The woman who had handed him the dive record at the lake the night before had doubted his veracity as a detective. In her words he had been dressed scruffily and appeared drunk. Marshall wanted to make clear to his boss that he had gone to Coniston straight from the pub but had not been drinking.

The same day, Thursday, 14 August, Home Office pathologist Dr Edmund Tapp arrived at Furness General Hospital in Barrow to conduct a post-mortem examination. In front of him lay the remains, partially re-wrapped with the packaging and rope. Aged 64, Tapp was an influential and respected pathologist and known informally as 'Eddie'. He was a courteous man with thinning white hair and spoke softly with a distinctive Lancashire burr. His bright eyes lit up behind glasses when he smiled, which he did often away from the autopsy room. For a time he collaborated with the renowned Egyptologist Dr Rosalie David, who established the Manchester Egyptian Mummy Project at the University of Manchester, which garnered a lot of public attention beyond academic circles. Tapp and David jointly edited two books in the 1980s and 90s and they appeared in a television programme performing an autopsy on a mummy.

Tapp was driven – how else could he return day after day to work that was rooted in trauma and tragedy? He did so with professionalism and a mellowness that allowed him to relate well to colleagues and associates. He was incredibly well thought of and respected and he was proud of his achievements.

Despite his public demeanour, Tapp was affected by the nature of his work. His son, Nigel, observed the man away from the stresses of the job. Speaking to me for this book, Nigel said, "I can remember when I was a kid my father screaming in the night, woken up with a nightmare. He saw some gruesome stuff. He just dealt with it, I don't know how, but he did."

This iron resilience had been shaped early. Tapp had been born in a tiny village on the moorlands of Lancashire in an unheated, damp end-cottage. They were years of economic uncertainty and Eddie suffered a devastating accident at the age of ten when he fell against a pot of boiling water and scalded his back and shoulder. He spent the next year in hospital and was allowed home only because the doctors believed he was about to die. His grandmother and sister nursed him back to health, however. The will to live and to work hard served Eddie Tapp well and it led to a distinguished career as a Home Office pathologist.

Now he focused his considerable professional attention on the macabre remains in front of him. Here was the dark canvas bag and the pull-cord. There was the piece of lead weight that diver David Mason had seen. It had been flattened and folded over a number of times; looped through it was blue plastic rope. He delicately opened the bag. Inside he found two loose pieces of wood and two pieces of elastic bandages. The package was still tightly bound so he loosened it further and untied the ropes enough to continue his examination. The first suggestion that he was dealing with human remains came when what appeared to be bones from hands and a number of teeth fell out. He opened the package further still and found the feet. They had become detached from the body.

Now the entirety of the remains was exposed. The body had a white, waxy appearance. Tapp noted it was in a state of adipocere, a condition which affects dead bodies that have been in water. The waxy substance is formed during the decomposition process and is caused by the breakdown of neutral fats in the body. The dead woman was wearing a blue babydoll-style nightdress popular in the 1960s and 70s and was tied in a foetal position. Rope had been passed around the front of the shins, around the back of the calves and the buttocks. The legs were tied across the front of the body and secured with a knot at the hip. A loose rope appeared to have been passed around the neck.

Observing the array of sophisticated knots used, Tapp could not recall in his lengthy career having encountered a body trussed up the way this one had.

He could see that the woman had suffered major trauma to her face. The lower jaw was recognisable but the main cheek-bones had been smashed and the teeth had been knocked out. Indeed, the facial bones had been fractured into fragments, some of which still had teeth attached. Loose in the package he found other facial fragments and teeth. The two largest fragments were from the side of the face, the zygomatic bones, and Tapp could see that one of the bones bore a sharp edge. He believed this suggested a cut to the face rather than a fracture caused by a blunt object. Tapp examined the woman's brain. It was difficult to say whether there had been any injury to the organ. He took photographs of the skull. Whoever had inflicted the injuries upon the woman's face had done so with considerable force. He believed it would have taken at least two blows to inflict such injuries and a heavy instrument with which to do so. A heavy instrument such as an axe.

The woman's left hand, too, was fractured. At this stage Tapp could only speculate, but it suggested she had tried to defend herself. She would have lost consciousness and died very rapidly after such injuries and had probably drowned in her own blood. There would have been considerable bleeding at the scene where the attack took place, Tapp noted.

He knew the facial bones would need to be pieced together if he were to consider what had happened to the woman. He knew exactly who would be the right person to perform the delicate act of reconstruction.

Tired from intense concentration, he concluded the post-mortem examination, cleaned up and left Furness General. He drove back to the home he and his wife Joan had built in Lostock on the outskirts of Bolton in Lancashire. He changed into shorts and switched off his thoughts by gardening with Joan in his landscaped half-acre.

In the hours after the body's discovery and shortly after Dr Tapp's post mortem examination, Cumbria Police briefed the media. Getting journalists involved swiftly was crucial in appealing for help from the public.

Speaking to TV reporters at Barrow Police Station, DCI Noel Kelly said, "From what we were told this morning from the post mortem, it would appear that this lady is aged between 20 and 30, five feet one to five feet four, with short, dark hair."

Kelly had a strong face and looked like a rugby player. He was dressed in a dark suit and tie befitting the grave nature of the moment. He appealed directly for help from the public. "Anyone who can give us some information as to anyone of that description who is missing, anything up to 20 years ago, please let us know," he said.

Very quickly the incident room's phone lines were red-hot with calls suggesting who the dead woman might be. Many names were historic missing persons the police already had on file. DC Marshall recalled, "It was a case of sifting through those to make sure every lead was followed up."

One name kept cropping up. A young woman who had been missing since 1976.

A Golden Age in Journalism

I picked up a copy of the previous Friday's paper and went to sit at my desk in the *Westmorland Gazette* newsroom in Kendal. It was early on the morning of Monday, 18 August. I unfolded the broadsheet paper – pages the size of movie posters – and stared at the front page, the crisp gothic-lettering of the masthead at the top. Staring at me were two of the biggest news stories in my five years working at the paper.

'Two die as 'copter crashes' was the secondary headline on the page. In any other week this story would have been the splash. My colleague Rachel Garnett had written: 'Villagers stared disaster in the face this week when a helicopter nose-dived and exploded into a fireball in a field just yards from their homes and the M6 motorway.' Two pages had been dedicated inside to the dreadful events.

And yet that wasn't the lead story.

The main front page headline in underlined block capitals

read: 'GRIM DISCOVERY'. The subhead read: 'Police launch body in bag murder inquiry' and there was a simple black and white map of Coniston Water with an arrow pointing to the location of the divers' discovery. The story was by our deputy news editor Mike Addison who had been tipped off by his diver neighbour, and read: 'A murder investigation has been launched after the badly-decomposed body of a woman was pulled by divers from the depths of Coniston Water.'

Mike had interviewed the divers and said police were treating the matter as murder, providing details of the victim's height and clothing, and confirming the belief that the remains could have been in the water for up to 25 years.

Mike's story looked back at another notorious 'body in the lake' murder from recent times when a woman's corpse was found in England's deepest lake, Wast Water, in 1983. The body turned out to be that of Margaret Hogg who had been missing since October 1976. In 1984, her husband, airline pilot Peter Hogg, was arrested for her murder. At his trial at the Old Bailey he was found guilty of manslaughter after it was established Hogg had accidentally strangled his wife during a violent argument. He was jailed for four years. Hogg had driven to the Lake District, rowed out in a small boat and pushed his wife's body – wrapped in a carpet – over the side.

The discovery of the body in Coniston Water had me gripped. It had been five days since the discovery. These were pre-internet days so unless you read it in a newspaper or heard about it on TV or radio you could easily miss a story, even something as big as this. And I had been on something of a news diet in Malta.

The *Westmorland Gazette*, which was launched in 1818, remains one of the oldest newspapers still publishing in the United Kingdom. The contributors to its letters pages include William Wordsworth, John Ruskin and Beatrix Potter, while *Confessions of an English Opium-Eater* author Thomas de Quincey was its second, laissez-faire editor. In recent times, the *Gazette* was the first publisher of the exquisite hand-crafted walking guides by Alfred Wainwright.

The offices were on Stricklandgate, the main street through the centre of Kendal. A stationer's shop on the street gave way at the back to a long, narrow open-plan office running all the way to space once occupied by the *Gazette*'s printing press. (This had been dismantled and removed by the time I joined the paper, with weekly editions now printed at Bradford.) First you passed through the advertising department before reaching the editorial department at the rear. The cacophony of ringing telephones and raised voices was an assault on the senses. I adored it.

Editorial consisted of pairs of desks lined in rows facing a blank wall. It was like sitting on an aeroplane with gangways either side of you. The space was divided invisibly into sections: the subs' desk, the sports desk, the news desk and the reporters' desk. It was a configuration arranged the previous year with the introduction of new computers and a revolutionary electronic diary and network of digital news baskets called Lotus Notes.

The Editor was John Lannaghan, who wore his hair in the style of his hero, Roxy Music singer Bryan Ferry. In his fifties, Lannaghan was a no-nonsense journalist from the west coast of Cumbria. He had an inscrutable manner belying a dry sense of humour. Being called into his office was a scary event. You never wanted to disappoint him. If you made a mistake, he would defend you publicly against external criticism while expecting you privately to learn and put things right. He had my utmost respect.

My immediate superiors were news editor Andrew Thomas and deputy news editor Mike Addison, both in their thirties. Yorkshireman Thomas was whippet-thin with a sharp analytical brain who was a stickler for clarity. "What does this mean?" he asked me once not long after I'd started. He was unpicking a nebulous paragraph I'd written. "If you don't know what it means, how do you expect your readers to?"

I learned a lot from him very quickly.

Addison was a keen fell runner from east Lancashire, six years older than me and a great mentor, especially when I was struggling to get my 100 words a minute shorthand as a trainee. He wore his hair over his collar, was warm and funny and enjoyed the quickfire newsroom banter. He was also a brilliant reporter whose hunger for a story was insatiable. Once he'd known the Coniston package was a body, he ran down the hill from his home to the *Gazette* office to write the story.

It had been almost five years since I started at the *Gazette* and I was now part of the fixtures. It was the newspaper I had grown up reading. I had been taken on as a trainee reporter in the summer of 1992, straight out of university. That autumn I spent five months near Hastings on the south coast at the training centre of Westminster Press, which owned hundreds of newspapers up and down the country including the *Northern Echo*, the *Bradford Telegraph* and *Argus*, the *Brighton Argus* and of course the *Westmorland Gazette*. Reporters from the *Financial Times* were also trained there. I shared a five-storey Edwardian terraced house on Warrior Square in St Leonards-on-Sea, a mile along the coast from Hastings. My room was in the attic. If you peered through the tiny window at an awkward angle you could just about see the English Channel. Each morning we walked along the promenade to a building that looked like an ocean liner had beached on the seafront. The art deco Marine Court was constructed in the 1930s to look like the then recently launched Cunard Queen Mary.

There were 40 or so of us on that year's Westminster Press course. Each day we crammed into a tiny lecture theatre for myriad lessons in libel, contempt of court, council reporting and newspaper writing. Interspersed were tiring lessons in Pitman shorthand and typing.

Each trainee was given a news patch and one afternoon a week we were sent out to find stories. Every Wednesday afternoon I caught the train from Warrior Square station and travelled a few miles up the line to the village of Battle. This, I discovered, was the true location of the bloody clash between the invading Normans and King Harold in 1066. The battlefield lay behind the impressive walls of Battle abbey.

At the end of the five months I had my qualifications in media law and government and I could type 40 words a minute. My shorthand, though, had stalled at 90 words a minute, ten short of the required 100 words, and it would take a further three months to hit the required speed to allow me to legally cover court hearings.

I arrived back in Kendal days before Christmas 1992. I was shown my desk in the *Gazette* newsroom, my Apple Mac computer and my telephone, and told to start reporting. And so my apprenticeship in news began.

I started my career at a time that may well prove to be the

last golden age of print newspapers. There was no internet, no social media and print newspapers, television and radio were the only sources of news. At a grassroots level, it made local newspapers like the *Westmorland Gazette* all-powerful: where else did the public learn what was happening in their street?

Newspapers were the place to go if you wanted a new job or to buy a car or a house. Advertisers pumped cash into papers like the *Gazette* to reach their readers while newspaper companies like Westminster Press looked on in satisfaction. Within a decade, however, all the money leaked to the internet as estate agents, employers and motor traders realised they could promote their services on their own websites.

But in the mid- to late-1990s, when I was starting my career, newspapers were thriving relative to today. Consequently, there were a healthy number of journalists employed in the *Gazette* newsroom. There were three journalists on the news desk, more than a dozen reporters, including specialists in farming, business and sport, four sub-editors, three photographers, plus a host of support staff and assistants. The advertising, circulation and accounts departments plus the graphic studio were all bursting with talented staff.

As I had grown up in Kendal, inevitably I knew a number of people at the *Gazette* including some of the advertising reps and Steve Barber, one of the photographers. I was one of a number of trainee reporters and we were well supported by the several older journalists who were generous in their encouragement.

One was Dennis Aris, who besides his general reporting duties, wrote a satirical column called *The Way I See It* in which he lampooned what he saw as the stupidity of local politicians and powerful people. He was a keen amateur musician, playing trombone in Ulverston Town Band, and I remember seeing musical notation he'd scribbled on the backs of planning agendas during interminable council meetings. For a time I sat opposite Deborah Kermode, who was a keen traditional Furness clog dancer and a member of the Furness Clog dancing group. She used to practise her clogging steps under the desk as we both sat typing up our reports.

Karen Barden was the *Gazette*'s talented chief feature writer. I remember her profile of a thriller writer called Jim Grant from Kirkby Lonsdale whose first novel was about to be published. During his weekly shop at Asda supermarket in Kendal, an old lady had asked him to reach her an item off the top shelf. Afterwards, his wife suggested a name for his character based on Grant's conversation with the woman: Reacher. Jim Grant duly became Lee Child and christened his hero Jack Reacher.

I eased back into work by opening the Everest of mail on my desk. There was an invitation to the London press launch of a new BBC television drama. It was called *The Lakes*, by Liverpool screenwriter Jimmy McGovern. It promised to expose the Lake District's underbelly of itinerant hotel workers, sex and drugs. Before the show had been screened it had already upset guardians of the Lake District's wholesome image amid fears of damage to tourism.

The invitation came to me as I wrote the *Gazette*'s arts and entertainments pages. I admired McGovern's writing on Channel 4 soap *Brookside* and police drama *Cracker*. If he were looking to write a gritty Lake District story he need look no further than the incident room at Barrow Police Station.

I put the date in my diary: Monday, 1st September.

Andrew Thomas told me I would be covering the Furness

district office that week while Deborah, the clog-dancing reporter, was on holiday. As Barrow was part of Furness, I knew I would now be leading the *Gazette*'s coverage of the Coniston Water murder.

I gathered my things, took one of the *Gazette*'s pool cars, a royal blue Rover Metro, and set off for the Ulverston office.

Barrow CID incident room.

By Monday, 18 August, detectives had received a list of 46 possible names from Scotland Yard's Missing Persons Bureau. Among them was a file on the woman whose name had come up consistently in calls from the public. She was now a focus for the investigators. Identifying the body would require matching the teeth with existing dental records. Armed with the name of the missing woman, DC Doug Marshall and a colleague visited her dentist on Abbey Road in Barrow.

Unhelpfully, the records had not been properly filed.

"They had a garage full of boxes of little dental cards," remembers Marshall. "And I remember sitting in my jeans in this garage with another officer all afternoon going through box after box. And it was typical, the last box I looked in, there it was."

Meanwhile, police divers had combed the bottom of the lake in search of clues around the lake bed where the divers found the body. They had set up sonar equipment. The Royal Air Force had also flown over Coniston Water taking images of where the body was raised, providing a photographic record of the lake's topography.

Detectives had now set up the main incident room, to handle calls and inquiries, at Cumbria Police's headquarters at Carleton Hall at Penrith in the north of the county. There were also satellite incident rooms at Barrow and Ulverston and a command post at Coniston to deal with direct lake inquiries. The investigation was gaining momentum.

The police knew they would have to formally identify the woman quickly. DC Marshall recalled, "There was a lot going on with the media and obviously one of the problems – and it's an inherent police problem with journalists – is to try and quell all the speculation until we have the facts."

4

Death Knocks

The *Gazette*'s office in Ulverston was in spacious rooms above Barclays Bank, in a handsome red sandstone building in County Square. I found myself sitting at Deborah's bank-manager-size desk peering across to the Coronation Hall. The Coro, as it is known, had special significance for me as it was here in May 1947 that Laurel and Hardy were given a civic reception. They had stood on the Coro's balcony and convulsed a large audience below with laughter. Stan Laurel was born in Ulverston in 1890 and he and comedy partner Oliver Hardy visited as part of a tour of the music halls. I'd loved the comedians since I was very little and had been a regular visitor to Ulverston over the years.

I took out my notebook and pens and flicked through Deborah's handover notes. It was Monday. I needed to produce stories to fill three change pages of the main edition by Thursday's deadline. This might not sound a lot. But bear in mind the *Gazette* was still a broadsheet paper, with huge, gaping pages, and took a lot of filling. I was expected to produce a front-page splash, plus leads for pages three and five. Each of these would be up to 500 words. There were down-page stories, sidebars and news-in-briefs to find and enough photographs for each page to be organised.

For a moment I froze. Where on earth should I start? The phone rang, jolting me out of my trance. I lifted the receiver. "Hello, *Gazette* newsroom" and I was off.

The phone never stopped ringing.

The mail piled up on my desk.

The ad reps from the room next door wore a trench into the carpet bringing me scribbled phone messages ('could you ring Mr so-and-so, he's got a story for you'; 'Mrs Thingy wants to complain about that story last week, can you call her back?').

Running the district office on your own is not for the faint-hearted. At Kendal I was used to juggling several stories at a time and feeling my editors breathing down my neck. But I was part of a team and we bore the pressure together.

Top of my newslist was the Coniston Water murder. The question I wanted to ask was: who was the dead woman?

The case had rapidly become a national story. Hundreds of reporters, photographers and television crews descended on the Lake District in the days after the body's discovery. Hotels and guest houses were swamped with requests at short notice from journalists for rooms. Reporters swarmed around Coniston Water and the Barrow area once it was hinted the victim was from the town. As the police checked missing persons files, reporters too were scouring old cuttings for long-forgotten cases to get ahead of the curve.

I picked up the previous days' editions of our rival paper, the *North West Evening Mail*, which was based in Barrow but had a district office in Ulverston. They put out six main editions (Monday to Saturday) compared to our one edition. They were able to go much deeper than we were and they were sitting on a rich archive of cuttings to draw from. Indeed, detectives visited the *Evening Mail*'s offices to trawl through back issues in their quest to identify the victim. The paper would see a spike in sales during its coverage over the coming days and weeks.

They had led their Thursday, 14 August edition with: 'POLICE LAUNCH MURDER HUNT – Divers discover body in Coniston Water.' All the information, including the quotes from the police, were the same as those in Mike Addison's report for us. As the case was fast moving in these early hours and days, the *Evening Mail* responded. The following day's headline was 'THE BABY DOLL MURDER' accompanied by a photo of police divers searching Coniston Water. It told readers that detectives regarded the "remains of a sixties-style baby doll nightie" as holding the key to the murder mystery which, the piece claimed, could be 25 years old. There were details of Dr Edmund Tapp's initial examination of the badly decomposed body. Police revealed that the woman was white and thought to have been in her twenties when she died, had stood between 5ft 1in and 5ft 4in, was well-built and had short, dark hair. Det Supt Ian Douglas confirmed police were hoping to use dental records to help identify her. But he admitted at that stage the nightdress was all detectives had to go on. There was also an interview with John Walsh, one of the Kendal divers who found the body, with the subheading: 'Diver feared to look at his gruesome find.' The divers had been praised by police for their public-spiritedness and the help they were providing police with their knowledge of the lake bed.

Walsh, however, admitted he wouldn't bring any strange bags up from the bottom of the lake in the future.

By that evening, Monday, 18 August, newspapers, including the *Evening Mail*, were naming a Barrow woman who had been missing since 1976 as the likely murder victim. Frustratingly, I was three days away from my deadline.

The woman's name was Carol Ann Park.

By the following evening, Tuesday, the *Evening Mail* had an interview with a member of Carol's family, who remained anonymous at that stage, but said they had given up hope of ever seeing Carol again a long time ago. The relative was quoted as saying, "We thought it was a bit suspicious at the time. We wanted to believe she had gone of her own free will but she didn't take anything with her, not even her passport."

The *Evening Mail* story revealed detectives had found an old news report from 1978 stating Carol might have gone to the Bristol area in search of her real mother, as Carol had been adopted. DNA samples were being taken from the body to compare with her blood relatives, while an attempt would be made to reconstruct the victim's face to assist Carol Park's dentist who was trying to use X-rays to identify work he had done on her teeth.

On Wednesday morning, my news editor at Kendal called. There had still been no formal identification of the body, but we agreed I would need to track down surviving members of Carol Park's family and speak to them. Her maiden name had been Price. She had a surviving brother, Ivor.

So, I drove from Ulverston to Walney Island near Barrow-in-Furness, a journey of 10 miles. I had an address for Ivor Price on Lord Roberts Street.

In the industry, a reporter's approach to a grieving family is known as a 'death knock', which might seem callous but accurately describes one of the necessary functions of the journalist. American writer Janet Malcolm wrote in her seminal book *The Journalist and the Murderer*, "Every journalist who is not too stupid or too full of himself to notice what is going on knows that what he does is morally indefensible." It is true, you are intruding into somebody's grief albeit acting in the public interest. I don't believe Malcolm's characterisation is the full picture. From my experience, grieving families are generally keen to see their loved ones commemorated in print; it is a form of validation that their lives mattered. During my career I have done a lot of 'death knocks' and was turned away on only a couple of occasions. In the 21st century it is done differently due to social media but in 1997 it literally meant knocking on somebody's front door.

Five years into my career death knocks never got any easier. I always had a sinking feeling in the pit of my stomach as I walked up to the house. One of the hardest had been two years earlier. On 23 January 1995 the families of two men raised the alarm when they didn't return home from work. At 1.30am Lancashire police visited the Morecambe garage belonging to Italian businessman Antonio Marrocco. Officers were not prepared for what they found. The 49-year-old had been bludgeoned to death with one of his own torque wrenches. The following morning the body of Marrocco's employee Paul Sandham was found in a field a mile from the garage. He had been stabbed 40 times. Detectives believed the killer had asked Sandham to test drive a car before killing him and returning to the garage to murder Tony Marrocco before fleeing with cash and Marrocco's gold chain.

I visited the home of Paul Sandham's partner first but she wasn't in, so I posted a note with my contact details through her letterbox. Then I went to Tony Marrocco's home where I hoped to speak to his wife. I knocked at her door but there was no answer. I went back to my car to consider what to do. I decided I would try again and this time, Geraldine Marrocco opened the door to me. I explained who I was and to my surprise she invited me into her home.

We went through to her living room. All the curtains were closed. Mrs Marrocco was subdued and looked like she had been crying. She sat in a chair and I sat on a sofa with my notebook open before me. Photos of her with her husband were on every surface. Twenty four hours earlier this had been her living room. Overnight it had become an unintended shrine to her husband.

Mrs Marrocco had no idea who would want to kill her husband. I hardly needed to ask questions: her emotions poured out and I scribbled down her words. She wanted me to put on record what a good man her husband had been. I could feel my own emotions rising, but I had to stay professional. I thanked her and left her with her memories. It was an interview I have never forgotten. Morecambe detectives eventually caught the killer, 24-year-old London-born man Terence Clifton, who had lived in Morecambe for a time. He was found guilty of double murder and sentenced to life in prison.

Now, I was faced with the same sense of trepidation as I prepared to visit Ivor Price.

Walney Island is a spit of land separated from Barrow by a channel of water and is reached by the Jubilee bridge, known locally as Walney bridge. Walney acts as a buffer between the industrial streets of Barrow and the storms of the Irish Sea. It is a pretty place with sand dunes, seabirds and tightly knit rows of terraced houses. Its attractions include Furness Golf Club and Walney Aerodrome. The Vickerstown area of the island was constructed by the shipbuilding firm Vickers at the end of the 19th century due to a lack of housing for workers.

Ivor Price's house was tucked away in one of the rows of terraced houses running down to the channel of water between Walney and Barrow. I parked the car up tight to the kerb. It was a sunny day and I was hot in my shirt and tie but I still slipped on my suit jacket; I wanted to look as professional as possible. I checked the address in my notebook to make sure I knocked on the correct door. I got out of the car with the same sense of dread I'd experienced at Geraldine Marrocco's home. With the sound of seagulls calling overhead, I went up to the house and knocked on the door. I looked around as I waited. *Nothing.* I knocked again. *Nothing.*

I'd learned to be persistent and my editors expected me to come back with quotes from Ivor Price. I got back in the car and drove around Walney to get a flavour of the place as it was unfamiliar to me. My colleague, Dennis Aris, lived in the Furness area and was a keen sailor at Walney. The car was stifling with the sun streaming in. I wound down the window. After a while I returned to Ivor Price's house and for a second time knocked at the door. I was about to leave when I heard movement inside and the front door opened. It was Mr Price, wearing a white shirt and a black tie. He was a gentle-looking man with short black hair and doleful eyes. I learned afterwards that, at 57, he was a retired worker at VSEL – Vickers Shipbuilding and Electrics Ltd – and had also been a scout for

Manchester City Football Club, spending his spare time watching the young footballing talent of Barrow. I introduced myself, expecting him to turn me away but he didn't. I learned that day the meaning of dignity. It was likely the body in Coniston Water was that of his sister who had been missing for 21 years. He had every reason to refuse to speak to me yet he remained courteous and briefly answered my questions.

We stood there on his doorstep and he spoke of the years of worry he and his family had suffered. At first he hadn't believed Carol was dead. He thought she had left to make a new life for herself. Now, as the week's events unfolded, he had started to fear the worst. There was a deep sadness in his face. I thanked him for his time, he closed his front door and I drove back to the *Westmorland Gazette* office in Ulverston.

Ivor Price was roughly the age of my father. Two years earlier I'd noted Geraldine Marrocco was a similar age to my mother. It was hard not to be affected by these intense moments of raw emotion.

Cumbria Police held yet another press conference that day. DCI Noel Kelly told reporters, "We are on the trail of whoever did this. Twenty one years on, I'm quite sure he or she thought they were safe and it was all over with." He paused, then said, "It isn't."

Privately, the pieces were falling into place. The police had a suspect in their sights.

We knew that the police would imminently announce the formal identification of the victim, but unfortunately it wasn't going to happen before we went to press on Thursday, 21 August. As a weekly newspaper this was incredibly frustrating. I could write my story based only on the known facts. In all likelihood our story would be out of date on Friday morning if the police made a formal identification after we were published. This was the major flaw of a weekly newspaper in those days before the internet.

Sitting at the desk overlooking the Coro, I scanned through my shorthand notes, checked everything against the known facts and began tapping the keys of my keyboard. The story with my byline would be the splash on the Furness edition and would be a down-page story on the front of the *Gazette*'s main edition.

This is what I wrote.

'Murder squad detectives are today (Friday) expected to name the woman whose body was discovered in Coniston Water last week.'

There was 'a strong likelihood she was Cumbrian and that the body had been in the lake at least 15 years'. This 'added weight to speculation that it could be that of teacher Carol Ann Park, 31, of Leece near Barrow, who disappeared 21 years ago'.

I reported that police were close to formally identifying the body using DNA samples and facial reconstruction but were reserving an announcement until it was confirmed out of respect for families potentially affected.

I filed the story and awaited the inevitable phone call from Kendal and questions from the newsdesk. When they were done, I sat back in my chair. It was dark outside; press nights were always late ones. I switched off Deborah's computer, took my car keys and switched off all the lights in the building (I was the last one there), locked the front door and walked to the car.

My mind was whirring. Had I got everything right? It was too late now to change anything.

5

Catching A Killer

Police formally named Carol Ann Park as the victim at a press conference on Friday, 22 August. They had known her identity since dental records in her maiden name of Price were recovered by DC Marshall. These, together with a file from Scotland Yard, had confirmed it beyond doubt.

Detective Superintendent Ian Douglas said specialist police officers would be helping Carol Park's now-grown children, Vanessa, Jeremy and Rachael, to recall the events of 1976 when their mother went missing. DS Douglas said, "We'll be asking them – and others – to unlock memories of a long time ago. It will not be easy."

Police had informed families of other missing women that the body was not their loved one. Douglas said it was difficult at that stage to establish whether the killer was familiar with Coniston Water. He said it was safe to conclude the killer must have used a boat from which to dispose of the body. Police were at that moment executing search warrants at properties across Barrow and tracing boats kept on the lake.

Although he would not speculate on who was responsible, Douglas told reporters it was not too late to catch Carol's killer, "There have been vast advances in forensic science in the past 20 years."

The newspapers did what they always do – pigeonhole, hang a story on a peg, invent a nickname. The case was a gift to a headline writer and the name was predictable and inevitable. Journalists borrowed the title of Raymond Chandler's famous 1943 detective novel and the sobriquet stuck. *The Lady in the Lake.*

The media attention swung back to Ivor Price. Shellshocked, he now knew what had happened to his sister. "We have had 21 years of things like this and I really could not face up to another 21 years. It has been a nightmare," he told reporters. "I could say it was the end, but it will probably be a far worse nightmare that I am going to face – I don't even know how I am going to cope with it."

Despite Cumbria Police's refusal to speculate on the killer, journalists had their theory of a possible suspect, based on their reading of old news clippings: Carol Park's husband Gordon.

With a live murder investigation under way, detectives Douglas and Kelly met Dick Binstead of the Crown Prosecution Service on the same day that Carol Park's identity was confirmed. Compelling evidence about Gordon Park's character and life had been uncovered in recent days. Binstead later wrote in a memoir, "I was presented with an overview of the evidence, but was left with no doubt that the officers believed that Gordon Park was the killer and that they intended to arrest him and charge him with his wife's murder."

Binstead raised no objection. He too believed all the evidence pointed to Park.

There was a problem, however. Gordon Park was out of the country, on holiday in France with his third wife.

6

The Macabre Jigsaw

Gordon Park had been on holiday in France since 23 July. He was a tall, fit-looking man who wore glasses and whose dark hair was thinning on top and greying at the temples. He had been a primary school teacher around Barrow for 25 years. Now at the age of 53 he was in semi-retirement and enjoying a slower pace of life. Since Carol had gone missing he had been married twice more and it was with his third wife, Jenny, that he was relaxing at a gite in the French province of Gascony. On Thursday, 14 August, they had been joined for three days by friends from Barrow, Paul and Ann Shaw and Ann's mother. The Shaws left for Carcassonne on Sunday, 17 August.

Park was oblivious to the news in the Lake District. But at home his children were worried the body might be their mother. His daughter Vanessa initially gave no thought to it but became concerned when she heard how long the remains had been in the lake. She spoke to her brother, Jeremy, on Monday, 18 August, who was having the same thoughts. Meanwhile, Paul and Ann Shaw cut their holiday short on receiving news their pet dog had died suddenly at home. They returned to Barrow to read speculation about Carol Park in the *Evening Mail*. Paul telephoned Vanessa out of concern.

Vanessa and Jeremy decided they should contact their father. Jeremy traced a phone number for Gordon. It was almost midnight on Tuesday, 19 August when he got through. He told his father he had some bad news. Jeremy said, "They think it's Mum and the police want to interview you." Jeremy would later recall his father's response was, "Oh dear, oh dear."

Park advised Jeremy, "Just tell them whatever you know, tell them the truth, we've got nothing to hide, help in whatever way you can."

"It was the start of a nightmare," Park later recalled. "The media wrongly reported that we were in hiding and that police were in France looking for us. In fact it just took us two days to get home."

Park did not rush home. He did not attempt to contact the police back in the UK. Neither did he try to make contact with his brother-in-law, Ivor Price.

Cumbria Police's investigation stepped up a gear. Detectives orchestrated their moves carefully. Paramount was ensuring the right flow of information to the media was properly controlled. DC Doug Marshall was conscious of an inherent tension between the job of reporters and what the police were trying to achieve.

"Our job is to try to quell the speculation until we have the facts," he recalled. "You don't want to jeopardise the investigation but of course there's a strong local public interest and for the police it's about finding a balance of what you can say and what you can't."

Marshall knew that until it had been confirmed that the body was Carol Park, it had been dangerous for the police to speculate. "Even at that very early stage, there were some big question marks over her husband and at the time when she was identified, he wasn't in the country, he was in France," he said.

The press conference to identify Carol Park on Friday, 22 August had coincided with an application to Barrow Magistrates for two search warrants. With Park out of the country, detectives needed permission to gather evidence without his consent. One warrant was to allow officers entry to Park's home, the other to gain access to the boat he kept moored on Coniston Water. The purpose of the warrants was "to look for and if necessary remove evidence in relation to the murder of Carol Park".

Armed with the necessary paperwork, police officers forced entry into Park's neat detached home at 34 Norland Avenue in the Hawcoat area of Barrow-in-Furness shortly afterwards that Friday. Officers broke in via a window at the rear of the property. The house was now a crime scene. Scenes of crime officers videotaped the inside of the house and photographed the interior of the single garage to the side of the house. Fingerprint and forensic experts spent many hours combing every room for evidence.

On Coniston Water officers meticulously searched Park's 19-foot Navigator-class sailing boat, called the Mrs J, which was moored at the southern end of the lake at Nibthwaite. Newspapers would report that police were studying records to try to trace a boat called Sail Fish, which Park was known to have raced on Coniston in the 1970s and which he was thought to have owned at the time of Carol's disappearance. Among those quoted in reports was Shirley Slater, a 64-year-old member of Coniston Sailing Club who recalled Park's considerable competency as a sailor. "We used to race on the lake on Sundays and he was very good," she told reporters. "He carried on coming after Carol disappeared and he brought his second wife. But soon after he met her he stopped coming because he was caught up in her."

It was reported that for two days police had done house-to-house inquiries in Leece. This was the pretty village east of Barrow where Gordon and Carol Park lived in the 1970s. Officers had also searched Park's former bungalow, Blue-stones, where he had lived with Carol. The current owner, Harry Furzeland, who had purchased the property from Park, was able to point out items left behind by the schoolteacher, including scrap lead piping and ropes.

As journalists continued to knock at Ivor Price's door in Lord Roberts Street, he continued to answer questions. He told reporters, "I feel very bitter towards the person who did this." Without naming who he felt was responsible, he said: "I have my suspicions but until a person is proven guilty, they remain innocent." He said, "I have every confidence that the police will bring the killer to justice."

And then he politely asked the journalists to go away and leave him and his family in peace and stepped back inside his house.

While still in France, Park made phone calls to a number of people including solicitors at a Barrow-in-Furness firm, Forresters. In a call to his friend Susan Shaw he sounded relaxed and his usual self, but was concerned about his daughter Vanessa. Despite the shocking news from home, Park had nevertheless decided to complete his holiday with his wife, Jenny. They left the gite on Wednesday, 21 August, stayed overnight in a guest house and yet another in the French port of Saint Malo on the night that police had broken into his home in Barrow. On 23 August they caught the ferry back to Portsmouth and eventually arrived back home in Norland Avenue in the early hours of Saturday, 24 August.

Since receiving news of Carol's body, Gordon Park had taken a total of four days to return home.

A breakthrough in identifying Carol Park as the victim had come after Home Office pathologist Dr Edmund Tapp conducted the post mortem. He had realised he would need assistance in reconstructing the facial bones. He knew exactly who could do the work.

Sixty-one-year-old Richard Neave was an expert in forensic facial reconstruction within the medical school at the University of Manchester, where Dr Tapp was attached to the Royal Infirmary as pathologist. Neave was a pioneer in his field and in demand. In 1988 he had done groundbreaking work in helping to identify the victims of the devastating fire at Kings Cross underground station in London. Tapp had previously called upon Neave's expertise in police forensic investigations. In 2001, Neave would become well known for reconstructing the face of Jesus for the television programme *Son of God* for the BBC and Discovery Channel. Tapp and Neave had both worked on Rosalie David's Manchester Egyptian mummy project.

Tapp went up to the facial reconstruction department but discovered that Neave was away. Caroline Wilkinson, who was a PhD student in her early thirties working under Neave, said she would be able to help using her mentor's techniques. (Professor

Wilkinson later became an eminent anthropologist and pioneer in the field of facial reconstruction. She currently leads Face Lab at Liverpool John Moores University and is perhaps best known for reconstructing the face of King Richard III in 2013 after the body of the much maligned monarch of Shakespeare's play was discovered under a car park in Leicester).

Tapp carefully presented her with the pieces of the skull and she set to work.

She recalled, "It was basically a case of sticking the pieces back together so that the skull looked as intact as possible so that photographs could be taken that he could use in his report.

"At the time – we don't do this any more – we used a sticky wax that held the pieces together so that it could be photographed."

When Wilkinson had successfully pieced together the macabre jigsaw puzzle, Tapp was able to examine the reconstructed skull as a whole. He was keen to identify incriminating signs of injury. Wilkinson remembers him looking closely at what appeared to be cut marks around the teeth.

Tapp thanked her. A clearer picture was crystallising. If his interpretation were correct this had been an act of violence beyond anything Dr Tapp had previously encountered.

7

The Arrest

Gordon Park arrived home late on the night of Saturday, 23
August. His life would never be the same again.

He and wife Jenny found journalists and camera crews
camped outside their home on Norland Avenue. They were at
the centre of one of the hottest unfolding news stories in the
land, their circumstances nestling besides reports of Princess
Diana's third romantic holiday of the summer with her
boyfriend Dodi Al-Fayed, the son of Harrods owner Mohamed
Al-Fayed.

The Parks were shocked to discover their home had been
raked over by police, who had taken away boxes of personal
items, including computer equipment and reams of paperwork.
Park also realised officers had confiscated all of his rope and
string.

Tired and no doubt distressed at the turn of events, he and
Jenny spent the night at home wondering what would happen
next. Their answer came the following morning at around 8am
with a knock on the front door. Detectives stepped into the

house. They informed a dazed Park that he was being placed under arrest on suspicion of murder. His rights were read to him. Park blinked at the detectives. Then he followed them out to a police car and was driven to Barrow Police Station.

DC Doug Marshall was waiting there, ready to interview him.

"Choices are like dominoes, one tumbling against the next and then the next until events go out of human control."

— Ann Rule

PART TWO

CAROL
PRICE

8

The Price Family

Carol Park went missing in the summer of 1976. Gordon Park would wait six weeks before reporting her disappearance to the authorities. And from the moment that he did report her missing, Gordon Park was in control of the narrative. He would retain a tight grip on that control for the next 21 years until her body was finally discovered lying trussed up in Coniston Water.

In 1976 Carol's disappearance was the latest in a series of devastating tragedies to blight the lives of her parents and brother Ivor. The sequence of events endured by the Price family was so horrible you would dismiss it as far-fetched had you not known it to be true.

Carol was adopted by the Prices after she was given away by her biological mother Elsie Saunders, a 24-year-old Land Girl in Bristol during the Second World War. Elsie went away to give birth to Carol on 18 December 1945 to conceal from her husband George, who was a soldier serving in Burma, that the child was the result of an affair. The baby girl was put up for adoption as far away from Bristol as possible to further cover

Elsie's infidelity: Barrow-in-Furness. And so it was that Stanley and Winifred Price adopted the baby girl, now named Carol, early in 1946.

At their home in the Barrow suburb of Roose they introduced her to their six-year-old son, Ivor. Ivor Price would recall, "It was the end of wartime and the next thing I knew was my father telling me one evening that when I got home he'd come to collect me at my grandparents. There was a surprise for me. And when I got home there was this young baby girl. She was lying in a wicker basket. And that was the first recollection I have of Carol."

The Prices had had another boy, Brian, who had died in infancy and in 1951, the couple had one more child, a daughter they called Christine. Carol was the only one of the Prices' children who was adopted.

Despite the controversy around her birth, Carol was doted on by the Prices and enjoyed a happy childhood. She showed musical talent early on and from the age of 12 played the organ at St Luke's Church in Roose. She was academically bright, passed her eleven-plus examination which took her to Barrow Girls Grammar School where she showed a facility for learning French and German, and came away with good exam results. Any ambitions of going to university, however, were dashed in 1963 when her father Stanley died suddenly. This event left Carol to pick up the pieces at home with her mother and younger sister Christine. So instead of days in lecture halls and libraries, Carol became a clerk in the finance department at Barrow Town Hall to bring a wage into the home. She was ambitious, though, and never stopped dreaming of an escape from the tight confines of Barrow-in-Furness.

She was a small, pretty girl, five feet two inches tall with dark hair. Those who knew her recalled a vivacious and outgoing young woman. The word everyone used to describe her was 'bubbly'. She was keen on walking – or 'rambling' – and camping in the Lake District, as well as youth hostelling. These were the early days of Beatlemania in Britain when the music was thrilling and the interests of the young mystified the old, especially in a conservative town like Barrow, so far removed from Swinging London. Carol might have been a long way from the buzz of the capital but she was living life to the full: dressing in the smart, fashionable clothes of the day and enjoying a full social life with friends around Barrow.

Soon she would be thrown into the orbit of a tall, dark-haired boy from Barrow just a few years older who would change her life forever.

It was true that Gordon Park was popular with the girls of Barrow but he seemed unaware of it. Ivor Price, Carol's brother, later remembered him as "the boy about town" whom several young women in the town were attracted to. Yet Park's own friends don't recall him having many girlfriends during his late teen years. His friends remembered that his first girlfriend was called Jennifer Shaw, known as Jenny. Fate is strange and Jenny had no idea in the early 1960s that she would eventually become Park's third spouse and discover, following a cycling holiday in France, that he was being investigated for murdering his first wife.

Park met Carol Price at a house party in Leece sometime in 1964 after both had been invited by a mutual friend. They recognised each other vaguely from their school days in Barrow and began chatting. Not long after they began courting.

"He'd got an eye for Carol and Carol went for it," Ivor Price recalled. He believed Carol was impressed by Park. Her friends said she quickly fell in love with him: he was strong, determined and resourceful.

By 1964, Carol's dreams of escaping Barrow were too strong to resist and she decided to leave her job at the town hall and pursue her academic ambitions. In September she went to train to be a teacher at Matlock College in Derbyshire, 150 miles south of Barrow. She and Gordon Park had not been dating long, but when she left for Derbyshire there was an engagement ring on her finger.

9

Boy About Town

Park was born on 25 January 1944, the second of three children of Sydney and Elsie Park, a solid Barrow family. Park had an older sister and a younger brother. His father was a painter and decorator by trade and owned a home decorating retail business selling paint, brushes, wallpaper and the like to DIY enthusiasts. He was successful too, with three shops in Barrow and one in Ulverston.

Importantly, Park's father was a keen sailor: he was a member of nearby Roa Island Boating Club and passed on his passion to young Gordon. The Parks kept a static caravan in the Lake District village of Torver close to the village of Coniston. Sydney Park would take his two sons sailing on Coniston Water in a 14-foot sailing dinghy. The young Park fell in love with the lake and sailing and pursuing outdoor activities generally. During his time as a pupil at Barrow Grammar School he met a group of friends, including Paul Shaw with whom he spent a few days in France in that fateful summer of 1997, who shared this passion for sailing and rock climbing. This was also the period in Park's life when he learned how to tie the sophisticated knots associated with sailing. A keen lifelong Scout, Park had an encyclopaedic knowledge of how to twist and thread a rope to achieve a specific effect, such as a bowline or a reef knot, each knot designed to perform a certain function.

By his teens, Park was experienced enough to go sailing with friends at Roa Island Boating Club and to take out his father's dinghy on Coniston Water. He would often go rock climbing in the Lake District, whose fells were a stone's throw from Barrow. Those who knew him say he liked to pit himself against nature.

It was as if he believed he could control the world around him.

In a strange twist of fate, both Gordon Park and Carol Price had encounters during the 1950s with water speed ace Donald Campbell and his race team.

In 1958, Park, his father and a friend were sailing their dinghy on Coniston Water when it capsized. They were rescued by Leo Villa, famous as the racing mechanic to both Donald Campbell and, earlier, his father Sir Malcolm Campbell. The incident was dramatic enough to make headlines locally and in national newspapers.

Many, many years later, Ivor Price would tell the story of Carol's encounter in 1955 with Donald Campbell. Speaking to the *North West Evening Mail*, Ivor recounted, "Donald Campbell came to our house, on the edge of Roose, with the politician Edward du Cann who knew my father. They came to see us on a fleeting visit. I remember Donald Campbell picking up Carol in his arms. It is strange to think that they both died in that lake [Coniston Water]."

When Park met and began going out with Carol Price he was

20 and working in his father's painting and decorating business. With Carol about to depart for teacher training college in Derbyshire, he did not hesitate in asking her to marry him. Perhaps this was an indication of his wish to keep his girl-friend on a tight chain while she was away from him. Given his tendency to want to control circumstances and events, this would be completely in character.

So Park watched his new fiancée pack her bag and set off for Matlock Teacher Training College in the gothic-looking Rockside Hall in the Peak District in the autumn of 1964. Park would send Carol a red rose every week and she would become upset if it was late in arriving. Yet even at this very early stage in their relationship there were signs of discord, red flags foretelling of a turbulent future.

Rockside Hall was a majestic former hotel perched high on a spot immediately above Matlock's one-time tram terminus. It had been built in 1860 as a hydropathic establishment for the improvement of Victorian visitors' health thanks to the fame of Matlock's restorative thermal springs. During the Second World War it had been used by the Royal Air Force, who had vacated it in the weeks leading up to Christmas 1945 after peace had been declared in Europe. Derbyshire County Council's education committee bought the hall from the owners, the Goodwin family, and set about turning it into a bustling teacher training college with the ballroom turned into an assembly hall and other large rooms converted into a gymnasium, common room and lecture halls. By the time Carol Price arrived, the college offered residential accommodation for up to 130 students and staff.

It must have been a jolt for Carol finding herself away from the town where she had grown up and which she had barely left during her 20 years. It was completely in keeping with her character that she quickly made plenty of friends thanks to her gregarious, vivacious nature.

Today we have the recollections of one of Carol's friends at Matlock College to gain an understanding of these early days in the relationship between Carol and Park. Early on, Rosemary Farmer was aware that Carol had a boyfriend at home in Barrow and she met Park when he attended the college's summer ball with Carol. She found him to be cold and intense and, disturbingly, with a tendency to control Carol. Farmer knew Carol was feeling emotionally insecure at the time, having only recently discovered she was adopted. Farmer never said this, but perhaps Carol saw in Park a father figure at a time when she felt some resentment towards her adoptive parents.

Rosemary Farmer was aware of cracks in Carol and Park's relationship, surprising given how new it was. Carol confided in her, revealing suspicions that Park was cheating back home in Barrow while she was studying in the Peak District. Farmer recalled that in their final year at Matlock, Carol had a particularly intense relationship with one of the college's lecturers.

At her 21st birthday back home in Barrow, Carol smiled widely, raising a glass of wine or sherry for the inevitable family photographs. She looked pretty in a sparkly powder blue sleeveless dress, her black hair short in a sixties style. In one of the photos, a handsome Park, his hair combed back in a Tony Curtis quiff, sits with a stony-look on his face and a cigarette in his hand. Rosemary Farmer remembered the party. She said Park was energised by plans he had for his future with Carol, chiefly his determination to build a family home. These were the seeds of what would become the bungalow Bluestones.

Nobody in 1966 could have predicted the infamy to descend upon the place 30 years later.

10

Bluestones

In the dying days of 1966, Gordon Park had purchased a plot of land with three stone cottages at Leece, a village just outside Barrow, and set to work converting them into a bungalow, which he would call Bluestones.

Leece was considered a step up from the poky terraced streets of Barrow. It was a quiet, secluded hamlet, not much more than a knot of homes clustered around a large pond called Leece Tarn. Once built, Bluestones stood on land next to the tarn and backed on to flat open fields that stretched as far as the eye could see. It was an exquisite spot.

Park gritted his teeth and set to work building his dream family home. He knocked down two of the cottages and Carol's uncle Arnold used some of the rubble to construct new walls around the bungalow that was to be built. Park, who was just 20, was handy enough to do some of the work himself, including some minor plumbing.

It was built mostly however through the efforts of volunteers as he called upon the services of many friends including school mate Paul Shaw and a local electrician who wired the entire property.

Park called the new bungalow Bluestones not because it was a pretty name but because of a memorable event during its construction. He had experienced great difficulty in levelling the plot of land before embarking on the work because of an unyielding jut of blue rock. As a last resort he blew it up with dynamite. Seeing tiny blue stones raining down gave Park the perfect name for his new home.

Iron-willed and ever practical, he worked round the clock to build a palace he said was for his bride-to-be and what he hoped would become a nest for their future family. But others were sceptical of his motives; some of Carol's friends believed it was an act of prideful peacocking.

Ivor Price believed Carol was impressed by Park's efforts and what eventually became Bluestones. He would recall, "It wasn't just an ordinary bungalow. It was a beautiful bungalow, built high above the town [Barrow] and the village of Leece and I'm sure the envy of many people at that time. And it was very beautifully laid out inside, very impressive."

Carol qualified as a teacher in June 1967 and returned to Barrow from Matlock College. Bluestones was almost ready. Yet, whatever thoughts were running through Carol's head about lesson plans and classrooms of young children had to be dispelled: her impending wedding day was now a month away.

She and Park were married on 28 July 1967 at Rampside Parish Church near Roose, a few miles east of Barrow in Low Furness. This lonely, centuries-old church sits on a small mound allowing a view of the sea and Piel Island. It is thought the church stands on one of the oldest religious sites in Furness, itself notable for its plethora of ancient sites of early worship. Chief among these is Furness Abbey, which dates back to 1123 and at one time was the second-wealthiest Cistercian abbey in the land after Fountains Abbey in Yorkshire. For centuries it was the church of the local farming community and generations of these families lie in the little graveyard nearby. Also buried here are the bodies of drowned sailors, including one who was laid to rest in a sea-chest after his corpse was removed from a ship blighted by the plague moored off Piel Island.

That summer, as the Park and Price wedding party made their way along the narrow path to and from the church, they were walking in the footsteps of Cistercian monks who had made the pilgrimage from Piel Island to Furness Abbey in the 12th century.

In a wedding portrait taken in the doorway of the church, Carol looks pretty in her white dress, her short black hair neat under her veil. Park is handsome, his dark hair swept neatly back in a quiff. He is wearing a dark single-breasted suit, with a waistcoat and a lighter-coloured tie. A white carnation is tucked into his left lapel. And he is smiling. In many family photos in the years to come, Park would adopt an unsmiling countenance, like that of a stern schoolmaster, which of course is what he would become.

It was a happy day of celebration. Many of Carol's friends knew how excited she was to marry Park, one recalling how much in love with him she was, how she would 'walk over coals for Gordon'. A number of friends believed she had married well. After all, Park came from a successful, well-to-do Barrow family who ran a successful and thriving business. When she was 16, and before she'd met Park, Carol had confided in her brother Ivor that she would never struggle in life because she was going to marry somebody with money. Thirty years later, that comment must have weighed heavily on Ivor Price's mind.

Park and Carol moved into Bluestones after the wedding. Aside from internal decoration, the bungalow was all but finished and they had the use of a bedroom, the kitchen and the bathroom. Despite early problems in their relationship, Park would later characterise the next two years as 'love's young dream'. They were in love, they had a lovely new home and they had no responsibilities to anyone but themselves. They both desired a family but they agreed they wouldn't start one until they were settled and Bluestones truly was complete.

And then tragedy hit, an event so shocking that it put the young married couple in a moral dilemma, but one to which they rose with fortitude and courage.

In light of what eventually happened to Carol, the events of April 1969 are incomprehensible. Carol's younger sister, Christine, had become pregnant at the age of 16 and gave birth to a daughter called Vanessa, born in March 1968. Christine would never reveal to anyone, least of all her family, who the father was. However, her on-off boyfriend from the time, John Rapson, who was a year older, claimed Christine had confessed to her that he was the father. Later he would also make claims that Christine was seeing other men during the time she was going out with him.

Events took a dark turn that April at the Roose Road home of Carol's mother, Winifred Price, where Christine and Vanessa were living. According to newspaper reports John Rapson attacked Christine after they had been having sex. He tied Christine to a chair and bit her on her breast before strangling her to death. Rapson attacked Mrs Price in the house but somehow she escaped to safety at a neighbour's house where the police were called. Rapson was later found guilty of murdering 18-year-old Christine and given a life sentence in prison. He served seven years before he was released on a life-licence in 1976. He appears to have gone straight for almost 20 years but by 1995 he had been sentenced to nine years in jail for sexual offences. He died in HM Prison Wakefield in August 2016 from an abdominal aortic aneurysm at the age of 66. But the spectre of John Rapson hung over the Price family for decades and would be a dark question mark in the investigation into Carol Park's disappearance.

The murder of Christine devastated the Price family. Her brother Ivor would later remember in particular the tragedy's impact on his mother and Carol. In the depths of despair in that final year of the sixties he could hardly have conceived he would have to endure the same piercing pain only a few years later for his second sister.

Christine's death left 13-month-old Vanessa without a mother. The question arose over who would now care for her. She had been living at her grandmother's house in Roose Road, the scene of Christine's murder, but Winifred Price was in poor health so it was clear she would not be able to raise the child. Ivor and his wife Maureen had just seen the birth of their third daughter and were unable to take in Vanessa, so Barrow Council took her into care and she was sent to Dunlop House, a children's home on Abbey Road.

Carol and Gordon Park stepped forward. They would adopt Vanessa, their niece, and raise her as their own daughter. Carol was now teaching at Victoria County Primary School in Barrow while Park was earning a decent living in the family business. They were in a position financially to help out. It was the right thing to do, Park would later attest, and he and Carol loved Vanessa dearly.

How terrible then that Vanessa Park, as she would become, during her life would lose not one but two mothers to murder. For now, though, the darkness of that second tragedy lay several years in the future.

The adoption of Vanessa was not plain sailing, however. Park maintained that everyone had agreed on the matter but when it went to court Ivor Price objected. Park later said Ivor Price agreed to his face but lodged the objection behind his and Carol's backs. Ivor Price always maintained that the deception had been the other way around, that Park and Carol applied to adopt Vanessa without telling him or his mother, Winifred.

It is unclear whose version of events is correct; the truth perhaps lies somewhere in the middle. The consequence, however, was that the adoption of Vanessa resulted in an estrangement of the Parks from the Prices. Many years later Park claimed Carol would not have anything to do with her brother Ivor.

At the time of the adoption Carol was pregnant and within a year of Christine's murder and now with Vanessa living with them at Bluestones, she and Park welcomed their first child into the world. A son, Jeremy, was born in March 1970 followed in May 1971 by a daughter Rachael. This significant change in the Parks' family circumstances must have softened their feelings and in 1974 they invited Ivor Price and his family to Bluestones for a meal and the rift was apparently healed.

The wider Park-Price family now entered what could be

described as a normal routine life. But time was ticking and dark clouds would soon begin swirling over Park and Carol once more and the sequence of events leading to murder would begin to click into place.

Park wanted more from life than working in his father's business. In those early years of the 1970s it was a difficult time in his parents' lives. Their relationship was disintegrating and would end in divorce. The breakup had a bad effect on Park and he was also feeling pressure at home with new responsibilities for three young children. Initially he went to work at textile manufacturer Lister's and then electrical firm Ferranti. His supervisor at Ferranti would later remember Park, who was now in his late 20s, as "sullen" and "condescending". He constantly appeared preoccupied and walked around the factory with something on his mind, she remembered, and the supervisor said that on one occasion he lost his temper and exploded in front of other factory workers, though nothing more is known about the incident.

Park didn't linger in these new jobs. He harboured ambitions to become a teacher like his wife. So, in 1972 he enrolled as a mature student at the Charlotte Mason teacher training college at Ambleside in the heart of the Lake District. The college was named after a renowned 19th century education reformer and writer from North Wales. In 1892, Mason established a training school for governesses and people who worked with young children. She called it the House of Education. One of Charlotte Mason's dictums was: "Education is an atmosphere, a discipline, a life." The school was originally based at a property called Springfield in Ambleside but two years later it moved to a handsome and palatial house called Scale How with generous grounds set back from Rydal Road, the main route through the town. It was here that Park would travel to and from Barrow each day to learn how to teach. Coming from the Ferranti factory in the industrial streets of Barrow, Park must have relished this exquisite lakeland setting.

This was also the period when his father, Sydney, newly separated from Park's mother, moved in with another woman. Hazel Butters would become Sydney's second wife. She did not warm to her new stepson Gordon. She found him flashy and materialistic, preferring to spend his money selfishly on new equipment for his boat or a new car rather than spoiling his family.

Park gained his teaching qualification and by 1974 was teaching at South Newbarns Junior School at Rising Side in east Barrow, a 10-minute drive from Leece.

Just as Park began teaching, Carol took a break from work so that she could spend time with their young family but when the children were old enough she returned to work. Her teaching colleagues of the time recalled her as being a dedicated teacher and mother. One, Isobelle Weaver, recalled that Carol was devoted to her work – it went beyond being simply a nine-to-five job. Mrs Weaver would also remember how proud Carol was of being a mother, taking baby Jeremy to a school sports day to show colleagues while she was on maternity leave.

Renewed relations between the Parks and the Prices meant that Ivor's daughters spent a lot of time with their cousins Vanessa, Jeremy and Rachael at Bluestones. The Price girls, Kay and Claire, loved seeing their auntie Carol but found Park stern. He would take them and his own children on sailing trips in the Lake District. Kay remembers he was a disciplinarian, stricter than her own father, which she attributed to Park's work as a schoolteacher. She later said, "Some of the things he did were a little bit scary."

She remembered mealtimes at Bluestones as particularly unsettling. To coax the children into eating their vegetables, Park would place an egg-timer on the table, upend it, and demand they had swallowed their food by the time the sand had passed through the glass. If they failed, he would slam a cane on the table. He detested chatter from the children during meals and would shout if they spoke while eating. "He was just very strict," remembered Kay. "But again, as a child, you just tend to think that's normal behaviour."

Claire Price was taught by Park at South Newbarns School. She found him as strict in the classroom as he was at Bluestones, shouting at the children to complete their work. "But we were in junior school and children are children, aren't they?" she remembered.

Kay Price never considered Park a loving person; she never witnessed any displays of affection, a comforting arm around the shoulder or a cuddle.

Nobody really knew what went on between Park and Carol in private during this time. Carol would later confide in friends and the true picture would only emerge many, many years later after her murder was uncovered. But it is apparent that Park systematically took control of every aspect of her existence, including her access to money. She effectively became enslaved within the marriage, shackled within the walls of the immaculate prison of Bluestones.

We have seen that early in their relationship in 1966 both Carol and Park had been unfaithful. Thirty years later it would emerge that Park and Carol had on one occasion mutually experimented with the idea of an open marriage and attended a wife-swapping party but Park admitted he had been ashamed and that neither he nor Carol actually had sex with other people on that occasion. Observers of the marriage would claim the major source of friction was Carol and Park's clashing personalities. Carol was outgoing and sociable, while Park was taciturn and controlling.

Over time and with the added pressure of a demanding family life, Carol began seeking attention from other men.

It began, really, when Carol started receiving a lift to work each day from John Wilkes, who was the headteacher of a neighbouring school in the village where Carol worked, Broughton Tower. He was a decade older than Carol and he and his wife were good friends with the Parks. He and Carol would talk during those car rides, although their conversations were never on personal matters. Although he and Carol never had an affair, Wilkes was the catalyst for Carol to start an affair with another man.

Park later believed the first man Carol had an affair with was a teacher she'd met on an Open University course, who lived locally in Barrow and was married with children of his own. Park confronted her and she left Bluestones to stay with her lover at the Swan Hotel, a smart whitewashed inn at Newby Bridge on the southern tip of Windermere. After two nights away, no doubt missing her children, she returned to Leece and was contrite, promising not to do it again. But within a month she had walked out once more. This separation too was short-lived and she soon returned.

Carol was in turmoil. She and Park would row constantly.

Kay Price remembered her auntie Carol coming to speak to Ivor. Carol would be crying and Ivor would try to console her over an argument she'd had with Park.

Carol's unhappiness caused her to stray again in August 1974. She was booked on an Open University course in arts foundation lasting a week at Keele University in Staffordshire. She did not have a university degree and in those days it was not necessary to possess one in order to teach, but she nevertheless felt she wanted to further her career and so sought additional qualifications.

She must have seen this week-long course as respite from the stifling atmosphere at home. On Monday, 12 August, sitting in her accommodation at Keele, she wrote a letter to Park. Her words were warm. She reassured him of her affection for him and that she would soon be back at the weekend. It is uncertain what her motives were for writing the letter. It was likely a sop to keep the peace at home, for before setting off she had arranged for her married lover to join her at the university in Newcastle-under-Lyme.

As it turned out she met a completely different man on the course.

11

A New Life

David Brearley was from the north east of England. As he and Carol spent time together that summer they opened up about their personal circumstances. Brearley told Carol that he was separated from his wife. He told her that he had a son called Michael. And although he had qualified as a teacher at the tail end of the 1960s, he had briefly been an officer with Durham Police before returning to the classroom.

Their mutual attraction developed quickly and soon Carol was telling him about her own life. He learned that she, too, was married but it was clear it was not a happy union because she had a boyfriend who was intending to visit her that week at Keele University. Brearley later said that no other man arrived.

The course came to an end on Friday and Carol and Brearley swapped addresses. There was a powerful mutual attraction between the two young teachers but at this stage their relationship was not sexual.

Brearley set off home for the north east. Carol packed her things and made the journey north to Leece, no doubt excited to see Vanessa, Jeremy and Rachael. But she was also returning to the reality of life with Park.

Park later remembered Carol was quiet when she returned. Had she had time to reflect on their relationship while she was away? Had this prompted her letter of reassurance? These questions no doubt ran through his thoughts.

Carol *had* been reflecting while at Keele. The experience had set her intention: she had resolved to get out of the marriage, as painful as that was to leave the children.

The strain between Park and Carol was evident beyond Bluestones. "I realised that things were very bad out there at Leece," Ivor Price later recalled. "Looking at the situation, I thought she was somewhat being dominated, controlled if you will." He knew his sister had a quiet nature, keeping her counsel and would not always articulate her thoughts if she had a problem. "But I gathered as I went out there that things were far from right. You could feel the atmosphere," he remembered.

Two weeks after returning from Keele, Carol walked out and moved into a room at the High Duddon guest house at Broughton-in-Furness, 18 miles away from Bluestones. Park drove her there. Carol stepped from the car carrying her suitcase and a hairdryer and walked solemnly on her own into the guest house. Vanessa, Jeremy and Rachael remained seated in the back of the car.

The scene was watched by the owner of the guest house, Anne Walker, who was to become a trusted friend and confidante of Carol's in the coming months. She was struck by Park's cold treatment of his wife. "I would have expected family goodbyes," she said, "and a hug from the children if she wasn't going to see them for a while. And I thought he [Park] was rather harsh the way he insisted they stay in the car."

Carol stayed with the Walkers for the next few months. During that time Carol never spoke directly about her broken relationship with Park, but Anne Walker detected hints in what she said. Concerned for the young mother, Anne would delicately ask questions. "I said, do you mean he hit you, that he was violent towards you?" she would later recall. "And Carol said, there's more than one way of being cruel. I've had to do things that I didn't want to do and I've always had to obey him because he thought he was in charge." Anne said Carol stopped short of saying Park had struck her but she sensed Carol was afraid he would become violent with her.

During this period Carol resolved to fight for custody of the children. This, though, meant she would have to meet with Park to discuss the matter. The Walkers could see that she was too frightened to see her husband privately so she made arrangements to meet at a pub in Broughton. As added insurance, she asked Anne Walker's husband Derrick if he would discreetly come to collect her from the pub in the event that things turned nasty with Park. Anne Walker recalled, "She said, I'll judge his mood and I might let him bring me back if I think everything's alright, but I'll know if I dare get in the car with him."

Over the course of a few weeks Carol met Park at the pub three times. Park drove her back to the guest house once. On the other occasions Carol felt safer returning with Derrick Walker.

Carol was starved of access to her children by a controlling Park during this time. A family photograph from this period shows Park with the three children, with longer hair falling over his ears in the style of the early 1970s and wearing a turtleneck jumper. He and the children are smiling but it is a poignant portrait not for what it shows but for what is missing: the children's mother Carol.

Ivor Price remembered how Park would only allow Carol to see the children under tightly orchestrated circumstances. "She had these visits to my mother's to see the children," he said, "and they were always supervised. And she wasn't allowed to see the children on her own apparently. And my mother says they'd go in the front room and Gordon was there… and it was very inhuman."

Anne Walker remembered, "There was nothing in life for her if she couldn't get those children back." Carol had suggested ways of her sharing custody with Park, Anne said, but Park rejected them all and continued to restrict her contact with them.

Shortly after Carol moved out to the guest house, she wrote to her new lover. The envelope fell through David Brearley's letter box in the north east of England soon after. Tearing open the letter, Brearley discovered what Carol had done. She'd written to him from the guest house and asked him to telephone her there.

Shortly after, he packed a bag and drove across the country from Middlesbrough to visit her in Broughton. Carol had asked to meet him in the village, away from the guest house. She no doubt wanted to avoid gossip, so she got into his car and they drove around aimlessly, excitedly talking. As Carol explained the breakup with Park and the powderkeg situation, Brearley became scared of what he might be letting himself in for. His attraction to Carol, though, was strong and his feelings were deepening. He made further visits to see her in November and

December, staying for a couple of days each time. He visited her at her mother's house in Barrow if it was a day to spend with her children. Brearley kept out of the way in one of the rooms at the back of the house while Carol spent her time with Vanessa, Jeremy and Rachael. All the while, these visits by the three children continued to be carefully manipulated by Park.

Nevertheless, the visits Brearley made from Middlesbrough gave them time to think and talk. He and Carol decided to set up home together. During visits to Brearley's native North East the couple began to look for a suitable house where they could move in together. She stayed at the Walkers' guest house until Christmas as she wanted to work out her notice at the school where she taught before she moved across to the North East to live with Brearley. Because she had become close to Anne Walker, Carol continued to keep in touch by telephoning her once a month and wrote the occasional letter. In the meantime, Carol had begun applying for teaching posts in the North East and successfully found employment at Sunningdales school in Middlesbrough for children with learning difficulties and began in the new term of January 1975. Typically with Carol, she soon established herself as a popular member of staff.

Importantly, Carol and David Brearley moved into their new home together: 21 Scott Road, Normanby, in Middlesbrough. Brearley's son Michael came to live with them. Michael was seven, a year older than Vanessa and three years older than Jeremy, and from the start Carol clicked with him, much to Brearley's relief. The breakup of his own marriage had affected Michael and he was keen that he and Carol built a new loving home for him.

The couple were very much in love. At last Carol had found

happiness and she didn't want it to end. She wanted to reinvent herself, to create a new life away from the shadow of Park. She continued to wear her engagement and wedding rings and began calling herself 'Mrs Brearley'.

Relenting, Park allowed the children to travel over to the North East to spend two weeks with Carol and Brearley during the school holidays. Jeremy Park would later recall these visits. He remembered Brearley: he wore a brown leather jacket and drove a distinctly 1970s car, either a Vauxhall Victor or Ford Cortina with wings at the back. Rachael, who was only four at the time, had hazier memories but remembered Carol giving them gifts: she received a set of Weebles, a 1970s egg-shaped toy that could not be knocked over, while Jeremy was given a toy plane and Vanessa a boat. She remembered playing with her new toy with Carol sitting on a thick white carpet in the Scott Road house.

Carol's new domestic happiness, however, would not last. Within weeks there would be fresh clouds circling as the date loomed for the court hearing to decide who got custody of the children.

Carol had asked Park for a divorce in September of 1974 and on the 13th of March 1975 she attended the custody hearing before magistrates in Middlesbrough. She hoped with all her heart that she would win and would soon have Vanessa, Jeremy and Rachael with her.

The hearing did not go well for Carol, however, and she would find the outcome heartbreaking.

The magistrates listened to what both Carol and Park had to say and found in favour of Park. Despite the impassioned testimony of Carol, the magistrates could not ignore the fact that it was she who had walked out of Bluestones to leave Park to raise the children alone. Many years later, Jeremy recalled, "Basically, my Dad put up a good case. He said, 'I've got family support. I've got school support, and it's better that the children should stay where they are'." Jeremy believed the magistrates made the right decision about him and his sisters because he believed his mother to be unstable at the time. It was his view that giving their father custody was the outcome he, Vanessa and Rachael would have wanted at the time.

But what the magistrates had not realised was that Park had lied under oath during the custody hearing. He claimed that he had not had an adulterous relationship during the same period that Carol was seeing David Brearley. In fact Park had been seeing the children's babysitter, Judith Walmsley, and he misled the magistrates because he didn't want that information to go against him when it came to the matter of awarding custody.

In the eyes of the court Carol had abandoned her children and it had been down to Park to pick up the pieces and care for them on his own. It was a deeply unfair characterisation and did not reflect the true nature of what had happened. It was a narrative that failed to expose Park's cruelty towards Carol and her desperate desire to escape the claustrophobic atmosphere at Bluestones.

Under the court's access arrangements Carol could see the children every other week and was allowed to have them for half of each school holiday. Carol was devastated. She could not cope with not being with her children and she began to take strong tranquillisers 'for her nerves', Brearley would later recall.

She may have been happy with Brearley – he was everything that Park was not – but the separation from her children was tearing her apart and she could not continue the way things were. Against her better judgement and putting her own happiness second, Carol knew she would have to return to Bluestones. So she took the drastic step of quitting her job as assistant teacher at Sunningdales with effect from 31 March, explaining to the headteacher that she was moving back to Cumbria, noting in her letter of resignation that "there are extenuating domestic and health circumstances", and apologised for the short notice. Brearley was not happy with her decision; they had not been together long, they had their new home together, and his son Michael was getting close to her. But he would have been a fool to have not seen the devastating toll the separation from her children was taking.

Carol picked up the telephone in Middlesbrough. She dialled the familiar number for Bluestones and took a deep breath.

Park answered.

She told him she wanted to come home.

12

The Easter Incident

It was the Easter holidays of 1975. Carol was back at Bluestones and Park loomed once more in her life. Crucially, though, she was back with her beloved children. The wrench from Brearley, as painful as it must have been, was offset by this fact. Park had brought to an end his relationship with Judith Walmsley.

Carol and Park talked at great length about their situation. Park no doubt wanted to know whether she was back for good; Carol must have struggled to provide an answer. On one hand she wanted to be with her children, but on the other, at what cost? Could she forsake David Brearley in the long run and return to a controlled life with Park?

Mystery surrounds exactly what happened towards the end of Easter. Park would recall it one way, Brearley another. It seems that Carol asked to see Judith Walmsley, no doubt curious to meet her husband's other woman. Park was resistant to the idea but Carol said she wanted to talk to Mrs Walmsley about Vanessa, Jeremy and Rachael. Despite Park's reluctance, he called Walmsley one evening and she came to the house to see

Carol. The three of them went into Bluestones' lounge to talk. Carol told Walmsley she would be leaving Bluestones again and asked if she would help Park with the children and treat them kindly. The way Carol spoke, Walmsley sensed that she was planning to leave Park for good. The meeting had been civil so far, the three speaking quietly but when Walmsley went to use the toilet, Carol began shouting and waving her arms about. She became hysterical, grabbing at items and throwing them across the room. Park later said he restrained her by taking hold of her arms and telling her to stop. Carol began kicking and writhing, urging him to release her and telling him, "You cannot hold on to me."

Park later wondered whether Carol's frenzied outburst had been triggered by the powerful tranquillisers she was taking. He would recall pinning her to the lounge floor and restraining her by sitting astride her, gripping her by the wrists to prevent her from hurting him or injuring herself. He shouted to Walmsley to call his friend Ernie Shaw. Upset by what she'd seen, Judith scrabbled to find Shaw's number in Park's phone book. She dialled the number and told Shaw what was happening. She hung up the receiver and went into the drive outside Bluestones to wait. When Shaw arrived he found Carol, who was crying, lying on the lounge floor with Park on top of her, trying to calm her. Park's father, Sydney, also came to the bungalow and asked Judith Walmsley to leave as he felt it was for the best.

There would be some dispute over who instigated the next event. Park claimed once Carol was calm that she called David Brearley in Middlesbrough; Brearley remembered it differently and maintained it was Park who called him. In any event, he drove across from the North East to collect Carol. He arrived to find a scene of chaos at Bluestones: he would recall shattered glass and soil and compost from broken houseplants strewn across the floor. He remembered that Park was amicable towards him and between them they helped Carol gather her things before Brearley and she climbed into the car and they drove out of Leece and headed back to the North East and their home in Scott Road.

That week of Easter 1975 had been a disaster. Carol had been so desperate to make it work with Park for the sake of being with her children. She had been prepared to give up her relationship with David Brearley, but once she'd been back within the confines of Bluestones and back in the company of Park himself, it had proved too much. Whatever had triggered Carol's violent explosion of emotion, be it the claustrophobic presence of Park, meeting Judith Walmsley, or the powerful medication she was taking, she had to get out.

Returning to Middlesbrough with Brearley allowed her to breathe once more but it was only a brief respite. As Easter rolled into summer, Carol became increasingly depressed over the separation from the children. Brearley could only look on; there was nothing he could do. Deep down he sensed their love would not keep them together. The pull of her children was too great. He knew the moment was coming when she would leave him for good. He began to grieve for what he was about to lose, a relationship that could have been wonderful.

The stress and worry of the separation from Vanessa, Jeremy and Rachael affected Carol's health and during July and early August she saw a consultant psychiatrist Dr Mosel Hudin. She told him that she was in a very unhappy marriage and felt that Park was constantly spying on her. Dr Hudin believed this marital discord had triggered her depressive illness and also believed that she had a personality disorder which meant that she was unstable in her relationships. He prescribed antidepressants and made a further appointment to see her in September.

She never kept that appointment because by that time she had made the decision to break up with Brearley and return to Barrow for good.

During the summer, Park renewed his relationship with Judith Walmsley but it would not last, for the final events in the life of Carol Park were about to unfold. Since Carol had gone back to Middlesbrough after the Easter meltdown, Park had allowed the children to once more stay with Carol and Brearley under the condition of the custody order. At the end of the visit, Park drove over to Normanby to collect the children. As they prepared to leave, Park and Brearley were cordially chatting when Carol started loading her packed belongings into Park's car to the surprise of both men. She said she wanted to return to Barrow, to stay with her mother. Brearley believed it was not a spontaneous decision from Carol; she had been thinking about it for some time.

So, unexpectedly Park found himself in the car on the journey back to Barrow with his three children and his wife. Park was at the wheel, his eyes on the road ahead, Carol in the passenger seat beside him and the three children snug in the backseat. As they motored back to Cumbria, he and Carol talked calmly about the events of the past months, the strains and troubles they'd experienced and, perhaps thanks to the gentle lull of the engine, or perhaps it was the soothing beauty of the Lake District, their old enmity melted away to the point where both agreed it was worth giving their marriage yet one more try.

Park's car never made it to Carol's mother's house in Barrow. Instead he swept off the main road towards Leece and pulled up outside Bluestones. He and Carol and their three young children took their things from the boot of the car and walked into their home as a family unit once more.

David Brearley would never see Carol again, nor receive a telephone call. Instead, they dissolved their relationship through writing. He posted the necessary documents to her to sign and they would be returned without resistance. She signed over the house to him and they sold the Ford Escort car that they had bought together.

Carol was torn in all directions. She had given an indication of where her mind was in a revealing conversation she had with the head teacher at Sunningdales in Middlesbrough. Although she had handed in her notice in March, she had continued to work there until the end of the summer term in 1975 although she failed to go into work on the very last day of term. To the headteacher's surprise, Carol turned up on his doorstep the following morning, now that the school had shut for the summer. He would recall that Carol was in turmoil and was uncertain about what she should do. She went into his home and opened her heart. She wanted to be at home with her children, that was clear, and she also confided that she was not as happy with David Brearley as she once had been. She told her boss that she found Brearley's son Michael hard to cope with. The headteacher listened and Carol thanked him and left with the weight of a life-changing decision on her mind. The headteacher never saw her again. He wrote a letter to Middlesbrough's County Education Officer explaining Carol's failure to attend work. He also described how David Brearley had been in touch with him during the summer holiday to describe a worrying event: apparently Carol had walked out of their Normanby home without explanation, and he'd reported her missing to the police. This triggered a call by a police officer to Bluestones to speak to Park, who had no knowledge of Carol's whereabouts. It eventually transpired she was at her mother's in Barrow. After this episode she returned to Brearley but it was only a matter of time before that final goodbye and the car journey back to Leece with Park and the children.

For Brearley this was the end of what he described as a nightmare. He would later describe the finality as "blessed relief". Brearley told the headteacher he had no desire to reignite his relationship with Carol.

News of Carol's reconciliation with Park and return to the family home reached the wider family. Many years later her brother Ivor Price reflected, "She made the ultimate sacrifice in 1975 by leaving the chap she was living with [Brearley], a decent guy, a nice home, a good future. She had to leave that because she loved those kiddies, these three children that were more important to her than anything else in the world."

Carol did not know it but she was entering the final chapter of her life. Within a year she would be dead.

13

A Trip to Blackpool

Park would later describe the weeks after Carol's return as "wonderful". He would say that they rediscovered their love for one another and enjoyed fun times together, especially with their close circle of friends.

Carol didn't work in the weeks up to Christmas 1975 but she was nevertheless keen to get back into teaching and at the start of 1976 she got a job at a local primary school in Askam-in-Furness a few miles up the coast from Barrow. Colleagues remembered her as happy and positive. It was the same wherever she worked. The caretaker would often sit and talk to her and never heard Carol speak of unhappiness at home.

All of this, though, was before the events upon which the Lady in the Lake case would pivot. For the next 21 years the details of Carol's disappearance would be governed by the account presented to the world by Gordon Park. That account would start to unravel when Carol's body was discovered in Coniston Water in 1997.

The fateful day, Saturday, 17 July 1976, was blisteringly hot.

It was the hottest British summer on record with highest temperatures reaching 35.9 °C. Newspapers and TV news bulletins were full of images of dry, cracked riverbeds and scenes of water rationing with families collecting buckets of water from communal standpipes in the street. The Government passed a Drought Act, appointed a Minister for Drought, Denis Howell, and designated parts of the country drought areas. In the Lake District, the long-hidden historic village of Mardale – flooded in 1935 to form Haweswater reservoir – emerged into view once more as the water level fell dramatically.

That day Park had promised to take Vanessa, Jeremy and Rachael on a day trip to the Lancashire seaside resort of Blackpool, famous for its sandy beach, amusement park and tower. Park would later claim Carol did not want to go and so he decided he would take the children on his own, leaving her at Bluestones.

Jeremy would remember his disappointment that morning. He thought he and his sisters were going to be taken for the day by both his mum and dad, a trip for all the family. The excitement of going on the rides at the funfair, of eating candy floss and fish and chips had quickly evaporated. He went into his mother's bedroom, he recalled, all excited. Carol was lying in bed. He tried to persuade her to go; school had just finished, it was the start of the summer holidays, always the most exciting part, with the long hot days that lay ahead. But she was quiet and withdrawn. She looked as though she had something on her mind. Despite his efforts to coax her into coming along, she was adamant about not going. "No, you go to Blackpool with Dad, you'll be OK," he remembered her telling him.

A trip to Blackpool was not Park's idea of pleasure. He would have preferred to go sailing, walking or climbing. A seaside funfair was more the sort of thing Carol enjoyed. But as she did not want to come, Park later recalled, and with three eager children, he packed their things for the day and drove off from Bluestones into the bright sunshine and headed for the M6 motorway to take them the 80 miles to Blackpool. The three children sat in the back of the car and listened to a portable radio that Park kept on the back shelf and for which he had specially bought batteries. They watched articulated lorries and cars rumbling alongside them as their father glanced in his rear view mirror, making their way to the coast, waiting for their first glimpse of the tip of Blackpool Tower piercing the skyline. The journey took around 90 minutes and the children were hot and overexcited by the time Park pulled their car to a halt and they were able to head off along the promenade in the direction of the amusements.

The funfair was exciting, overloading their senses with screams of terror and laughter from the rollercoasters, and smells of hotdogs and candy floss. Park took Vanessa, Jeremy and Rachael around the park, hoping to tire them out through excitement and activity. They rode many of the rides, including the famous Wild Mouse which throws the occupants of little rodent-like cars around a rickety rail precariously high off the ground.

Another reason Park had taken the children to the resort was to visit an exhibition about *Doctor Who*, BBC Television's hit children's science fiction drama, which had been on TV screens since November 1963. The first Doctor had been played by William Hartnell; in 1976 when Park took the children to the exhibition the role belonged to the boom-voiced and curly-haired Tom Baker wearing a floppy hat and yards-long scarf. He and previous Doctor Jon Pertwee had both created excitement and mayhem in 1974 and 1975 when they'd visited the exhibition dressed in their outlandish costumes accompanied by their on-screen companions.

Park, Carol and the children all enjoyed the show – it was a highlight of their week, sitting down on Saturday evening, eating fish and chips, to watch the latest episode.

The exhibition was on Central Promenade yards from Blackpool Tower. Outside was the Doctor's famous blue police phone box, a time-travelling machine called the TARDIS. Emblazoned over the exhibition's doors were the words: 'BBC TV Exhibition. Defy the Daleks! Visit the TARDIS'.

Park and the children wandered around the exhibition that day. When they approached a display of the Doctor's arch-foe the Daleks and heard their notorious chilling robotic catchphrase: 'Exterminate!' Rachael became terrified and ran to hide behind Park.

The children loved the day. It was only the second time they had visited Blackpool. The previous occasion had been to visit the resort's famous autumn illuminations which were strung along the promenade under the gaze of the tower.

Tired but thoroughly satisfied, the children climbed back into the hot and stuffy car. It was time to go home. Park slid his key into the ignition, turned the car northwards and set off for home.

When they arrived back in Leece that night they found nothing untoward at Bluestones, according to Park. They walked inside and found the bungalow as they had left it, untidy as normal.

But the bungalow was empty. Carol had gone.

There was no note, Park later remembered. He reasoned that she could not have gone shopping as he had been using the car. Had she nipped to the village shop she would have returned within five minutes of their arrival from Blackpool. He was perplexed, he later claimed.

He went into his and Carol's bedroom and found her engagement and wedding rings lying on the small dressing table. This struck him as odd. Yes, she had previously slid off her rings and slammed them on the kitchen table out of anger during a heated argument with Park but she had always returned them to her fingers and had never abandoned them in the house and gone off, ever.

"Where is Mummy?" Jeremy remembered asking. He later said his father became upset. Jeremy asked if he ever cried. "I am crying now," Park told his little son.

As puzzling as Carol's absence was, Park later said, he had pressing matters to consider: emptying the car, making a meal for the children before bathing them and reading bedtime stories before they went to sleep. It was only then, tired and with a moment to himself that he said he was able to stop and think about Carol properly. As well as there being no note, the telephone had not rung to say where she was. It did not occur to him to pop out and ask the neighbours if they'd seen her. A call to Ivor Price might have eliminated the possibility that she had gone to her brother's, but Park did not lift up the phone because he claimed he did not think Carol was close to either her brother or mother.

He would later state that he did nothing about his missing wife, instead adopting the attitude that 'if you wait, you find out'. And so he went to bed where he later claimed he could not sleep, lying awake wondering about his wife, waiting for her to telephone. His mind played over the possibilities and the most likely one, he told himself, was that she was in bed somewhere with another man. He was not worried about Carol's safety because she could look after herself. She could, he reasoned, attract other men and therefore would be looked after.

He was, he later claimed, hurt and bewildered.

14

Vanished

On the day that Carol Park vanished, I was two months shy of my eighth birthday.

I am the same age more or less as the Parks' adopted daughter Vanessa. I was born in September 1968 at Helme Chase Maternity Hospital in Kendal, 35 miles from Barrow-in-Furness. At the time, Kendal was part of the historic county of Westmorland before it was absorbed into Cumbria.

Mum worked as a telephonist at the local telephone exchange and then night shifts on reception at Westmorland County Hospital (where German Dadaist artist Kurt Schwitters died in 1948). Dad was a sales rep for the brewery Bass and spent his working days visiting pubs and working men's clubs across the Lake District. During school holidays in the 1970s he would take me and my brother on his calls, park his company Ford Cortina outside a hotel and leave us reading comics while he went inside to meet his customers. He would later appear with crisps and bottles of 'pop' with straws sticking out of the necks.

We became familiar with the Lake District's towns and villages as Dad navigated the Cortina around the winding country lanes, which always left me feeling car sick. Dad would stop at a red phone box and call Mum to let her know what time we'd be home for tea.

We lived in a former council house at 66 Castle Grove in Kendal. It had been my paternal grandparents' house. Mum and Dad bought it after Dad lost his mum the year before I was born in order to care for my elderly grandfather who lived with us. It was a handsome stone-built semi-detached with wonderful views of Kendal Castle from the back bedrooms. Our next-door neighbour was a printer at the *Westmorland Gazette* and every Thursday night he would pop a copy, fresh off the press, through our letterbox. I was always first to scoop it from the mat in the morning. I loved the smell of the crisp pages and the inky smudges they left on my fingers. This was one of the seminal influences on my decision to become a journalist. Interestingly, Alfred Wainwright, the famous guidebook writer whose books were published by the *Gazette*, had also lived at Castle Grove when he first moved to Kendal. He lived at number 19, a neighbour of my grandparents. Dad – a child at the time – recalled seeing him heading to work as borough treasurer at Kendal Town Hall.

My memories of the summer of 1976 are of long hot days playing outside with friends. I was oblivious to the events unfolding in Leece and Barrow. The matter had received very little newspaper coverage in Barrow and would not warrant a mention in the *Gazette*.

I was a reporter at the *Westmorland Gazette* when I first heard the name of Carol Park.

The day after Carol went missing, Sunday, 18 July 1976, Park was visited by friends, Malcolm and Angela Short. They found him outside Bluestones doing some work on his car. They asked how he and the family were and Park told them Carol had gone, taking nothing with her. He said Carol had left her rings as well as her purse and handbag. The couple noted that Park seemed irritated and annoyed. He told them that Carol had given him no indication she was leaving. He invited them into Bluestones but they decided not to as they felt he had enough to think about at that time, chiefly the children. As they left, Park gave them the impression he was hopeful of a telephone call imminently with news of Carol.

In the days and weeks after she disappeared, family and friends would cast their minds back to the last occasions they had seen Carol. It was strange because there had been no hint she intended to leave.

In the weeks before she vanished, she had bumped into Derrick Walker from the High Duddon guest house at Broughton-in-Furness. She'd told him she wanted to speak to his wife Anne: she explained that she had come back to Park for good and hinted that things were worse than they'd ever been. She promised she'd contact Anne over the summer.

But she never did.

Anne Walker remembered this period, of how Carol cropped up in her thoughts and she would think, "Oh we haven't heard from Carol".

Ten days before Carol vanished, both Ivor and Maureen Price saw her at the performance of a children's show at Barrow Town Hall on Duke Street. The Prices spoke to Carol during the interval. With the excitement and chatter of the crowd ringing in his ears, Ivor Price was worried about his sister. She seemed subdued. It crossed his mind that she might be depressed, though she never said as much.

Maureen would recall seeing Carol again for a final time on the last day of the school term, Friday, July 16, the day before the Blackpool trip. Carol had called with some money for a Christmas savings club. During their conversation, Carol said she would bring a card for Ivor and Maureen's daughter Kay's 14th birthday, which was imminent. She also told her niece that she would bring a present for her. Carol never came with the card or present.

Had she intended to once more abandon her children, her home and her marriage to Park, Carol certainly hadn't given that impression to her work colleagues at Askam school. One of the teachers remembered her discussing lesson ideas for the new term in the autumn. The caretaker remembered speaking to her on that last day of term. The blackboard was wiped, books and pencils put away and the excited children released for the summer. Carol, too, seemed excited as she described her plans to take her children to Blackpool.

A neighbour of the Parks in Leece, Mary Robinson, remembered seeing Carol in good spirits outside Bluestones one morning. She thought it was a Saturday, the start of the summer holidays, which would make it the 17 July, the day of the Blackpool trip.

One day that autumn, there was a knock at Ivor Price's door on Walney Island. Standing on the step was Gordon Park. He told Ivor that Carol had gone missing. Ivor asked how long it was since she'd disappeared. "Six weeks," Park replied.

Ivor was shocked. "Six weeks!"

"Has this matter been reported to the police?" he asked his brother-in-law.

Park said that it hadn't.

Stunned, Ivor ordered him to do it immediately.

Yet, Park did not go to the police. In an act that would strike many as strange, he chose to go to his solicitor first to report Carol's disappearance.

PC Alexander Miller was on duty at Barrow Police Station when the telephone rang. He answered the phone and it was a solicitor who said he was representing Gordon Park of Leece. He was formally reporting the disappearance of Park's wife, 30-year-old Carol. Miller took down the details, hung up the phone and went to speak to his superior, Police Sergeant Bill Lawson.

Lawson later recalled, "It was just odd, you know, it's a bit queer, this. What the hell's he got his solicitor for? Does he not want to speak to us for some reason? It was a hell of a long time for somebody to be missing before you reported her."

Park later explained he did not know what the formal procedure was for reporting a person missing and as he was in the habit of taking legal advice, he had felt he should do it through his solicitor.

Officers Miller and Lawson drove out to Leece to speak to Park at Bluestones the same afternoon. He told them the story of the trip to Blackpool and how she was gone when they returned. The officers made notes, listening patiently as Park explained she appeared to have left her handbag with money and also her rings.

Pocketing their notebooks, Miller and Lawson explained that officers would need to conduct a search of Bluestones and its outbuildings. Park nodded and the officers left. Shortly after, two plain-clothes detectives from Barrow CID arrived to ask Park more questions and then looked around the bungalow. They opened drawers and turned over the contents, they opened cupboards and inspected the shelves. They looked at Park's paperwork and took away documents they found interesting. They looked around the garden. Carol was nowhere to be found.

Sergeant Lawson returned to Bluestones another day in an effort to speak to Vanessa, Jeremy and Rachael. He was keen to know whether their mother had said anything to them before the Blackpool trip. This might prove important testimony, Lawson reasoned. When he arrived he was surprised to find Park on the driveway waiting, as if he'd been expecting him.

"What do you want?" Park asked.

Lawson explained he wanted to speak to the children.

"Sorry," Park said, "you can't see the children. In any case, they're not here. The children didn't speak to their mother."

Sgt Lawson said goodbye and left Bluestones with the feeling that Park wasn't telling him everything.

The police felt uneasy about Park's story. For a number of days after his cold exchange with Park, Sgt Lawson scoured the fields around Leece to see if there were any spots that had been dug up, looking for signs of a shallow grave. "I had a gut feeling that something wasn't right," Lawson admitted. But he found nothing and without hard evidence and without a body, there was nothing further the police could do.

Over the coming weeks the two CID officers returned to see Park with fresh questions, a process that would last until Christmas.

There was press interest in Carol's disappearance, naturally. In December, Barrow Police felt a public appeal should be made in an effort to find her. The CID officers organised for a photographer from the *North West Evening Mail* in Barrow to visit Bluestones to take a picture of Vanessa, Jeremy and Rachael standing next to their decorated Christmas tree. It was used in a story in which the children were pleading: 'Mum, please come home for Christmas.' Jeremy found the photograph incident traumatic. He later said it was the first time someone had suggested his mother was not returning.

The article appeared in the *Evening Mail* on Monday, 20 December with the headline 'Leece woman missing for six months'. It began, "Three Leece children are hoping for one thing this Christmas – a message from their mother." The photograph showed Vanessa, eight, Jeremy, six, and Rachael, five, all smiling sweetly to the camera, hanging decorations on the tree.

The reporter outlined the background to Carol's disappearance on 17 July. Park was quoted, "We are all very worried. If only she would let someone know she was all right it would be bearable. I hoped she would at least send the children a Christmas card. It is more than six months since anyone has heard from or seen her."

The article continued, "Police, too, are anxious to trace her whereabouts. They say that in spite of extensive inquiries they have been unable to locate her and they request anyone who may have seen her, or who knows anything at all, to contact them."

The final word was given to Park, who told the reporter, "If only she would let someone know she was alive and well, for the children's sake."

It was interesting that Park used the phrase "let someone know she was alive". He had always maintained that he believed Carol had gone off with another man. Was it a subliminal slip? Did he really know that she was dead?

Carol never returned. The police had no evidence a crime had been committed. They effectively wound-down the inquiry. Park occasionally bumped into one of the CID officers around Leece and they would talk about Carol's disappearance.

Despite the absence of incriminating evidence, police told Gordon Park that if a body were ever to be found, he would be the main suspect.

All final sightings of Carol were pinpointed to the 16 July, that last day of the school year. The following day, Saturday, 17 July, was when Park claimed Carol had refused to go with him and the children to Blackpool. Park insisted that Carol had walked out on them while they were in the seaside resort. Aside from Park, only their son Jeremy could confirm having seen Carol on the 17 July.

There would be one person, however, who would come forward and claim to have seen her after 17 July, miles away from the Barrow-in-Furness area. During the 1970s, the woman had attended the same church as Ivor Price and knew Carol, but not as well. They had once lain in adjoining beds in a hospital ward and had been friendly but things had cooled after the woman believed Carol had become snobbish, thinking herself a cut-above after marrying Gordon Park.

The woman was going on a caravanning holiday with her husband and had pulled into the Charnock Richard service area on the M6 in Lancashire. As she approached the toilets, she saw Carol Park walking towards her with a Hunter handbag slung across her shoulder. The woman said Carol turned her head to avoid eye-contact, clearly not wishing to engage in conversation.

The date was Saturday, 17 July 1976. The same day as the Parks' trip to Blackpool.

When she read about Carol's disappearance in a newspaper that autumn, the woman contacted Ivor Price to tell him of her sighting. He urged her to report it to the police.

It would take 29 years to unravel the mystery of this sighting.

"A person often meets his destiny on the road he took to avoid it."

—— Jean de la Fontaine

PART THREE

GORDON PARK

15

"Here we go again"

Sunday, 24 August 1997. 1.06pm. Barrow Police Station.

A tired and shellshocked Gordon Park sat opposite the two detectives, one of whom was DC Doug Marshall, their hands resting in the no-man's land of the desk between them. Sitting beside Park was his solicitor Mike Graham, of well-known Barrow-based legal firm Forresters.

One of the detectives asked Park about the day his wife Carol went missing, a day more than 21 years earlier. He asked Park what his thoughts were after learning she had disappeared.

"Here we go again," Park said.

The detective asked Park if he'd like to explain what he meant.

"Not really," Park replied. "But I will. It's when a wife walks out on you and you don't know where she's gone or why. It's just awful."

The detectives listened, Park's voice captured as evidence on a recording device.

Park continued, "You're totally disorientated."

During the interview, Park made little digs at the police: "No doubt you've got experts who can tell you all about that. It's not very good and it's happened before. And so it's, as I say, 'here we go again'."

One of the detectives asked Park to confirm if these were his feelings at the time.

"And you wonder what's going to happen this time," Park continued. "And if there's going to be another boyfriend, or what."

DC Marshall studied Park and his reactions to their questions. Today, more than a quarter of a century later, Marshall's impressions are seared into his memory. He remembers Park as being a "strange character, difficult to know, aloof, a sense of superiority about him". He also noted Park had a tendency to answer questions with sarcasm.

From the off he believed Park was lying. "This was just an attempt to hoodwink the police," Marshall recalled. "He didn't like to mention [Carol] by name. He didn't talk about her as you would expect somebody who was in what he described as a loving relationship. The way he spoke about her was more as a commodity than as a person."

Later the same day Park broke down in tears when discussing his children and Carol's relationship with them.

"Why am I crying?" he asked the detectives. "It's bloody stupid, crying."

One of the detectives asked if he was OK.

"I'm going to be OK," replied Park. "Stupid fucking questions."

The detectives asked why he hadn't returned from their

holiday immediately after news of the body. Park had a pragmatic answer. They had accommodation bookings and a reservation on the return ferry. By the time it was looking likely to be Carol's body their holiday was at an end anyway. They'd cleaned their gite, strapped their bikes to the roof rack, hooked up their luggage trailer and spent two days travelling back to Cumbria. In their overnight accommodation, Park had switched on the television news. It had been shocking to see a report with footage of police combing their home and removing black bin-bags of evidence.

Detectives asked Park what he'd thought had become of Carol during the long years before her body was discovered.

"Every possible speculation," he replied, "until I wore myself out speculating and decided this was pointless. I would stop and get on with my life, and I suppose there were other people who would say, 'What a callous bastard that is'."

Had Park considered the possibility that his wife had been murdered?

"Every possible speculation," Park told the detectives. "Every scenario, every infinite little thread of everything. Anything, everything, until you finally wear yourself out and say stop."

And then he told detectives, "I would like to know who put her there. You have sat there and flown your flag. You have also looked me in the eye and you say I have killed Carol. Fair enough. Thank you for the honesty. At least we know where we stand, but I look you in the eye and I say also I did not kill my wife. I do not know what happened."

Police questioned Park for 36 hours. In all that time Park made no admission of guilt. DC Marshall was struck by Park's personal control shown during the interviews. "His demeanour was quite intense," Marshall recalled. "He wasn't showing a lot of emotion."

The detectives were keen not to jump to conclusions. They knew people reacted differently in such intense situations.

"There's no guide book for how you should react," Marshall said. Nevertheless, the police had been carefully building evidence against him. Detectives were building a picture of the sort of man Gordon Park was. They were establishing what had happened following Carol's disappearance.

In the months after Carol vanished in 1976, Gordon Park continued with his life as though nothing had happened. He was now effectively mother and father to his three children. He continued to teach and dedicated his weekends to the children, relying on the help of family and babysitters for support.

Vanessa, Jeremy and Rachael remembered Park's disciplinarian side, the strict rota of jobs he insisted they carry out and the stern talkings-to he would deliver if they misbehaved. Vanessa remembered that in more extreme cases, to establish which child had committed a misdemeanour Park would line them up and smack them to draw an admission from the culprit, although Vanessa's recollections of a cane being used were not shared by Rachael.

Park passed on his love for the outdoors and took them to the village shop in Leece to buy sweets. He taught Jeremy how to sail in a small craft on Windermere. In his spare time he built a large dinghy almost eight feet in length and capable of holding a number of people. He named the craft 'The Big O', inspired by the nickname of one of his favourite singers, Roy Orbison.

He rarely discussed their mother's disappearance with

the children. It was a subject banished to the fringes of their existence.

All three children went to South Newbarns School, where Park taught, although he ensured none of them were in his class. The head teacher at the school, Keith Harrison, remembered Park as intense and focused. Harrison recalled two school trips with Park, one learning to canoe on Windermere, the other youth-hostelling in Coniston with 30 children. During a walk around Coniston Water, Park remarked to Harrison how beautiful the lake was and commented, "It is really deep, you know."

16

Mum and Dad
Rolled into One

Time marched on. The children were growing. Two years after Carol vanished, Park decided something needed to be done. On 22 November 1978, he filed a petition for a divorce from Carol. He cited her desertion from their marriage as grounds. The legal process was protracted and on 15 August 1979, three years after she vanished, the decree absolute came through. Gordon and Carol Park were divorced. In her absence.

Park did not stay single forever. He began a relationship with a local woman, Catherine Sillars, and they were married on 18 July 1981. She had five children of her own and when they moved into Bluestones the walls almost buckled under the pressure of 10 people under one roof. Park's second marriage would be short-lived and he later described the attempt to blend two families as "maximum domestic disharmony".

After Cath Sillars and her brood left, Rachael Park recalled, "Collectively, we got our life back." She and her siblings were now teenagers and moved on. She remembered she could rely on her father, whether for advice about her first boyfriend or first menstruation. "For all those sorts of things I went to Dad, and he was wonderful," she said. He was "Mum and Dad rolled into one".

Despite this, there was still something missing. Jeremy later put it this way, "I was growing into a teenager but I still grew up feeling inadequate because you've only got one parent."

Rachael believed that in not discussing their mother Park was protecting their self-esteem, shielding them from Carol's reputation. She admitted her father's attitude was if you couldn't say something nice about a person you were better off saying nothing.

Eventually, perhaps haunted by the mystery of their mother's disappearance, Vanessa, Jeremy and Rachael resolved to search for her. If she was out there, they wanted to find her. So they began in 1992 by acquiring a copy of her birth certificate. Jeremy later admitted they didn't know what else to do beyond asking around for her. They didn't ask the police for help as they had formed the view that Cumbria Police couldn't tell them anything.

Time marched on once more. Jeremy went to university; Rachael started a new life working in Switzerland. In 1991 Park sold Bluestones, 15 years after Carol had gone missing. He was now in a new relationship with the woman who would become his third wife, Jenny. They had known each other from a time before Park met Carol. Now they had rekindled their friendship and fallen in love. He moved in with Jenny, a house she had bought after her divorce. She had two teenage children, Jane and Stuart. Two years later, in 1993, they were married. Jenny was Mrs Park number three.

Park encouraged his son to be self-sufficient the way his own father had done with him. When Jeremy returned from university there was no bedroom for him in the new house. Park said they could convert the loft: he would tell him how to do it but he wouldn't help him. So for two months over the summer Jeremy worked on the project his father had set. Each morning, Park went to school and left Jeremy to it. Jeremy jacked up the roof using a hydraulic car jack and realigned the beam to allow for the conversion. It was a huge responsibility for Park to lay on his son's shoulders: one error and the whole roof could come crashing down. Each night, Park would return from a day of teaching, relieved to see the house in one piece. At the end of the summer, Jeremy returned to university and because it wasn't quite finished, Park completed the job. When Jeremy returned at Christmas he had a new bedroom in which to sleep.

Ever practical, Park would spend some of his spare time away from teaching doing odd-jobs and DIY for friends, refusing payment, taking the satisfaction he derived from the work and the beer or wine he was given as gifts. One of the jobs he completed during this period was some tiling at St Paul's Church, in Barrow, where he and Jenny worshipped.

Jeremy would remember these early years of his father's marriage to Jenny as happy ones. He remembered the new family home being filled with music as Park played guitar and Jenny piano. Jane and Stuart, Jenny's children, were also talented musicians. Park and Jenny performed music in old people's homes in the run-up to Christmas.

As well as visiting church, Park found himself drawn in a new spiritual direction. Along the coast from Barrow was a Buddhist temple at Conishead Priory near Ulverston. Park began to visit and discovered a newfound peace through meditation.

In the summer of the following year, 1994, Park decided it was time to retire from teaching. He was 50, still a young man. Jenny would continue to work full-time at a school, which meant they would still have to take their summer breaks during the school holidays, something that would explain why they were in France three years later when the body was discovered in Coniston Water.

On the day that Park left South Newbarns School the moment was recorded for posterity. Dressed in a polo shirt, he smiled for a photograph, surrounded by many of the children he had taught. Three years later, that photograph began appearing in newspapers for a much darker reason.

17

A Domineering Bully

Time was running out. Detectives had held Park for 24 hours and were granted permission to hold him a further 12. The officers had not taken a break and were surviving no doubt on caffeine and adrenaline.

They quizzed Park intensively about his marriage to Carol and probed him about her illicit affairs and her relationship with David Brearley. They delved into his second and third marriages. They asked him about his love of outdoor pursuits, of his passion for sailing, his boats, his enjoyment of climbing and of his proficiency and knowledge in the tying of knots. And they asked him pointedly about the day Carol went missing. They were keen to know why it took so long for him to report her missing. They pinpointed the exact date he told authorities: Saturday, 4 September 1976. Six weeks after she vanished. Throughout this line of questioning, Park was reluctant to say anything beyond telling detectives to refer to his original police statement in 1976.

The clock was ticking, time was running out. Marshall and his colleague knew it was crunch time: charge him or release him.

At just before 8pm on Monday, 25 August, the detectives went into the interview room where Park sat with his solicitor. They told him that he was being charged with the murder of Carol Ann Park on or about Saturday, 17 July 1976.

Park looked at the detectives. "I am innocent of this charge," he told them.

On the evening of Monday, 25 August, reporters gathered outside Barrow police station for a short press briefing. Cumbria Police press officer Tara Vallente, a former journalist I knew from her days on the *Lakeland Echo*, a rival Kendal paper, made a statement: "At ten past eight this evening a man was charged with the murder of Carol Ann Park. He will appear before Barrow magistrates tomorrow morning at 10am. I can confirm that that man is Gordon Park."

A small mob gathered outside Furness Magistrates Court on Abbey Road in Barrow early on Tuesday, 26 August. Reporters, photographers and television crews had been waiting at the rear of the courthouse even longer. They were expecting Gordon Park. Their patience was rewarded at 9.35am with the arrival of an imposing white security van carrying him. Police tightly guarded the court's rear gates as the van swung in and photographers raced to flash their cameras against the blacked-out windows in hope of capturing an image for the later edition newspapers.

Inside, the court's public gallery was packed and the press bench was bursting with reporters from newspapers, news agencies and television and radio. Among them was my colleague Deborah Kermode, now returned from her holiday and back on duty at the Ulverston office of the *Westmorland Gazette*. Bespectacled Park was escorted into the dock by two security guards to whom he was handcuffed and stood before the magistrates. He was dressed smartly in a white shirt and grey tie and trousers and a maroon blazer. He was taller than the two security guards at his side and he appeared to tower over them. He blinked as he looked around the courtroom. He appeared edgy but remained calm. He could see his solicitor Mike Graham at the bench in front of the magistrates, ready to speak for him. Next to Graham was Dick Binstead, for the Crown Prosecution Service.

The clerk of the court asked Park to give his name and address. In the only words he would speak during the hearing, he replied, "Gordon Park, 34 Norland Avenue, Hawcoats, Barrow-in-Furness."

The charge against Park was read out – that he had murdered his wife Carol Ann Park on 17 July 1976. Prosecutor Dick Binstead outlined some of the details that were known about the case. The magistrates listened intently. This was a special sitting of the court, called because of the charges that had been brought late the previous night against Park.

Solicitor Mike Graham said Park "strenuously denies the allegation" and indicated that he would be making no application for bail. In any case, prosecutor Dick Binstead would have objected to any such application on the grounds of a substantial risk Park might interfere with the potential witnesses, who presumably included Ivor Price and Park's own children. The CPS also considered the possibility Park might abscond if released. For Park's own protection magistrates believed custody was a better place for him at that time as they considered there was also a potential suicide risk. Prosecutor Binstead knew, anyway, that further along the judicial process Park was likely to be released on bail as he was a man with an unblemished character and no previous convictions. He was also unlikely to abscond as his family and roots were in the Barrow area. Consequently, magistrates remanded Park in custody for a week until Tuesday, 2 September, for the next hearing.

The whole first hearing lasted no more than 10 minutes. Park turned in the dock and was taken away by the security guards, his wrists still manacled to theirs. Reporters quickly spilled out of the court to file their copy.

Looking on from the public gallery was Ivor Price.

Hundreds of people lined Dryden Street at the back of the magistrates court in the hope of seeing Park being led into the security van. They were disappointed as guards led him discreetly from a holding cell to the van out of sight of the crowd. Police orchestrated a smooth exit by synchronising all nearby traffic lights to green, and Park was whisked away behind blacked-out windows.

Gazette reporter Deborah Kermode mingled with the crowd afterwards. A number of them were parents of children who had been taught by Park at South Newbarns Junior School until his semi-retirement three years earlier in 1994. She also noted in her report, which appeared in the *Gazette* that Friday under the headline "'Lady in lake' husband on murder charge", that standing on the sidelines behind the court was the vicar of the parish in which Park lived, the Rev Christopher Jenkins of St Paul's Church, where Park had done the tiling work years earlier.

After Park's hearing, Dick Binstead visited Barrow Police Station where Det Supt Ian Douglas, the man heading the investigation, was bullishly stirring his team. They'd done an incredible job so far of compiling evidence in the manic days since the discovery of Carol Park's body, enough to convince the Crown Prosecution Service to bring charges against Park. Now DS Douglas wanted his team to make sure their man was put away for good.

"We've charged the bugger, now let's go out and get the fucking evidence," he instructed his detectives, who were dispersed in the belief they had enough to convict Gordon Park. "Ian's words were, and were intended to be, flippant and amounted to no more than a request to 'dot i's and cross t's'," recalled Dick Binstead in a memoir he wrote years later.

Meanwhile, Gordon Park was on his way to a cell at Preston Prison in Lancashire, his new home for at least the next seven days.

Despite the confidence and ebullience shown by Det Supt Ian Douglas, within the Crown Prosecution Service doubts had already begun to seep into the thinking of experienced prosecutors. Was there enough evidence to convict Park?

The events of those late days in August were shocking and emotional for the family and friends of Carol Park. Reflecting later on those dark times, Ivor Price recalled, "When the newsflash came on the television, we had just come back from holiday in Austria."

Maureen, Ivor's wife, remembered, "[Ivor] said, 'that's our Carol', and I said, 'don't be daft', and he said, 'it is'."

What a dreadful series of traumas Ivor Price had endured in a lifetime. He had lost two sisters to murder. In more recent times he'd lost a daughter to leukaemia and eight weeks later his mother had died of a broken heart. He would tell anyone who cared to listen: his mother's dying wish had been to see Carol again. Ivor was a devout member of St Mary's Church on Walney Island and had often helped others through work as a bereavement counsellor. Now he found himself taking support from the church and the wider community and he remarked, "I never thought the day would come when I could use the counselling myself." His strong faith was what was keeping him going, he said.

Anne Walker, the Broughton-in-Furness guesthouse owner, had had the same initial thought as Ivor Price when she saw news of the body. "I thought, 'this is it, this is Carol'," she later remembered. Anne was one of the many people who called Cumbria Police to suggest the name of Carol Park.

Ivor Price said, "I believe that Gordon Park put her in that lake. He knew Coniston like the back of his hand."

Anne Walker said, "We'd always suspected it had been a nasty end for Carol. Pretty certain who was responsible."

In the days prior to Park's return from France, detectives had spent two intensive days and evenings interviewing Jeremy Park in Scotland where he worked. They asked about his childhood and his father's boats. He told detectives he'd had a good childhood, that his father had been affectionate and fun. Jeremy Park felt officers were trying to build an image of his father as a 'domineering bully'.

Detectives wanted to take DNA samples from Jeremy and his sister Rachael to help identify the body. Rachael was abroad and would not be able to return to the UK for some time, but Jeremy travelled to Barrow on the morning of Saturday, 23

August. At the town's police station he gave his blood sample. The sight of the needle and the blood caused him to faint.

Jeremy provided a written statement over the course of three days in the week that followed.

Rachael Park lived in Basel, Switzerland, with her boyfriend. They were in the process of moving apartments when she heard the news. She was unable to return to the UK until Monday, 25 August. She was unprepared for the media circus in Barrow. She was met at Manchester Airport by family friends who drove her to Cumbria. They met Jeremy in a lay-by and she switched to his car with her suitcase.

There were up to 40 reporters and photographers, some with stepladders, encamped outside the family home in Norland Avenue. There was even a van selling fish and chips to the hungry journalists.

"Getting into the house was a nightmare," she said. "We went through a neighbour's house and climbed in over the back fence."

The following morning Rachael was interviewed by police. Detectives asked the same questions, focusing on her childhood and memories of her parents. She had difficulty recalling much as she had been so young at the time. The questions went on for hours across four days. The officers noted her answers and presented her with a written statement. She asked for parts to be altered and the process was resumed. She later claimed officers tried to put words in her mouth and consequently she refused to sign the statement until it was exactly as she wanted it.

Jeremy and Rachael felt defensive towards the police. The charge against their father was ridiculous. They knew him to be a straight, honest man, his reputation unblemished.

"We all took our lead from Dad," Jeremy recalled, "and thought that if we complied with the police investigation and volunteered information, everything would be fine."

He, Rachael and Jenny believed Park would sail through the police's questions and be released without charge. He later admitted the naivety of this belief.

Jeremy broke down when he heard his father had been charged with murder. Over the years, of course, he and his siblings had considered the possibility their mother might be dead. "That someone else might have done it – *yes*; that she'd gone off and come to harm – *yes*," Jeremy recalled. "But that Dad had done it – *no*."

Now, confronted with such a terrifying possibility, the Park children and Jenny began to question whether Gordon Park had murdered Carol. But at every turn, they thought of the man they knew him to truly be, and dismissed it.

18

A Young Mother

Media scrutiny on Norland Avenue intensified. This was an evolving news story and newspapers were eager for more detail to feed their hungry readers. At the eye of the storm, though, the Park family found the attention excruciating. Rachael Park later recalled, "All these crazy articles were being written in the media. It really felt as if you were being raped in public."

It was another tragedy that eventually shifted the media's attention in the early hours of Sunday, 31 August. Reports began filtering through of a terrible car crash in an underpass in Paris. Travelling in the vehicle were Diana, Princess of Wales, and her lover Dodi Al-Fayed. Both were dead.

Monday, 1 September 1997.

I caught the early train from Lancaster railway station to London Euston. The journey was a strange, sombre affair. I was lost in thought the whole journey. I stared out of the window at the scenery: early mist-covered fields and backs of houses, retail units and offices, dimly-lit roads, all flashing past. I turned to the newspaper lying on the little table in front of me, re-reading the words I'd already processed several times already. I was coming to terms with the news that had shocked the world 24 hours earlier. The day before I had come down the stairs of our Victorian terraced house to see the headline on our Sunday paper: DIANA DIES IN PARIS CAR CRASH. My wife and I sat in our pyjamas blankly watching the television news, tears rolling down our cheeks.

My train rolled into Euston and I streamed onto the concourse with the throng of passengers yanking wheeled cases behind them. I was heading for Soho for the press screening of the new BBC television drama, *The Lakes*. It was written by Jimmy McGovern, a brilliant screenwriter noted for his fearless and provocative dramas.

The opening scenes of the first episode were fast-moving and hard-hitting, depicting the character of Danny Kavanagh, a petty thief and gambling addict fleeing the psychological and physical confines of Liverpool for the expansive landscape of the Lake District in search of new beginnings. After the screening there was a press conference. I sat with the pack of reporters, scribbling shorthand notes in my pad. The actors included newcomer John Simm, who played Danny, the role that would set him on the road to stardom.

Stepping into the bright sunlight afterwards, I passed a London tourist gift shop with cardboard masks of members of the Royal family tucked into a rotary display stand. Among them were Princess Diana faces smiling back at me. I knew I would never forget that moment.

The next day, back at the *Gazette* in Kendal, I wrote a news story about the upcoming BBC drama. It appeared on page two of the *Gazette* that Friday, 5 September, headlined: 'Primetime TV drama stars Lakes'. I also wrote a long, personal opinion piece about the show and the reaction it had received from certain quarters in Cumbria. This longer piece was published the following Friday, two days before the first episode was screened. In it I praised the grittiness and portrayal of the underbelly of the Lake District's itinerant hotel trade. The programme painted a picture of Cumbria that the county's tourism guardians wanted to keep hidden. It appeared under the headline: 'The darker side of the Lakes'.

There had been a wave of concern, given McGovern's track record for writing dramas about drug addiction and murder, about the programme being made in Cumbria's picture postcard setting, which brings in millions of visitors each year. Apoplectic were the area's hotel and caterers' association along with the moral guardian pressure group the 'Friends of the Lake District'. I loved the programme. I knew it was edgy and would upset many. But I knew it showed the side of the Lake District not seen by visitors seeking out Beatrix Potter or Wordsworth sustenance.

Shortly after my piece was published, I was at my desk in the newsroom in Kendal. My phone rang; I answered.

A voice: "Hello… It's Jimmy."

My brain whirred.

It was Jimmy McGovern. He thanked me for what I'd written. He read the *Gazette* every week. He'd based *The Lakes* on his own experiences. As a young man he had worked at the Prince of Wales Hotel in Grasmere and had fallen in love not only with the Lake District but also a local girl, Eileen, who would become his wife.

Two years later, in 1999, I met McGovern when he taught a screenwriting masterclass at a hotel in Bowness-on-Windermere. I interviewed him on the lawn overlooking the lake. Our conversation at one point touched on the Lady in the Lake case in Coniston. He had followed it closely and included a storyline in *The Lakes*' second series, which was shown in January and February 1999. In these episodes, a cheating head teacher of a small Lakeland primary school kills his wife and takes her body out to the middle of a lake in a rowing boat and pushes it over the side.

In September 1997, the nation mourned Princess Diana for weeks. My abiding memory is of seeing her sons, Princes William and Harry, walking shellshocked behind their mother's coffin. In that moment you could see this was a family tragedy: two young boys had lost their mother at the age of 36.

Another young mother, taken too soon.

19

Forensic Detail

As the police continued their investigation during August and September of 1997, they brought in a number of experts to interpret the evidence they had gathered.

Chief among this evidence was the knotted rope used to secure the bag and packaging in which Carol Park's body was found at the bottom of Coniston Water. Police had also recovered copious examples of ropes and cords looped and tied in various knots from Park's Norland Avenue home.

There was one man, a forensic scientist whose knowledge and expertise in ligatures and knots, to whom the police turned: Rodger Ide.

That autumn, Ide was in his mid-fifties with a reputation as a forensic science investigator stretching back two decades to the late 1970s. His brilliance in analysing arcane evidence not only in ropes and knots but also in fire, had led him to regularly give evidence in court, usually for the prosecution. Over the years he would investigate and give evidence at some of Britain's highest-profile murder cases, among them the conviction of Michael

Stone for the brutal murders of Lin Russell and her daughter Megan and the attempted murder of Lin's other daughter Josie in 1996. He would also present evidence at the inquest into the suicide of mass murderer Dr Harold Shipman after examining the ligature with which the serial killer had taken his own life.

A week after the body had been discovered, Ide spent some time examining the cords, twine and rope presented to him by the police. He closely inspected a short length of twine threaded through a pinafore dress at least 14 times to then be pulled tight to enclose the body within the makeshift packaging of a duffel bag. The twine had been tied in knots and the loose ends had been neatly trimmed, possibly by using a pair of scissors, in a process that Ide considered extremely meticulous.

To begin, Ide concerned himself with the ropes, cords and knots directly associated with the body and package recovered by divers from Coniston Water.

Carol's body had been encased in a rucksack and Ide discovered that the draw-cords had been secured using figure-of-eight knots. He found further examples of sophisticated knots: half-hitches applied to a length of buff-coloured string wrapped around the body and a taut over-hand knot tied at the end which Ide believed had been used to prevent the string from loosening.

Ide looked closely at a further cord that featured a sheet-bend, an essential sailor's knot used for uniting separate knots of varying sizes. There were also examples of eye-splices, a method for creating a permanent loop, or 'eye', in the end of a rope and involves splicing together loosened strands. Again, it is a technique commonly used by sailors. Other knots he discovered included bowlines and reef knots.

Ide was particularly struck by examples he found of heat-sealing on some of the ropes and cords, a process to prevent rope from fraying because this was not a technique commonly practised unless by someone proficient in the use of ropes.

Detectives were thrilled with Ide's conclusions. They knew that Gordon Park was a frequent and competent sailor. They also knew he had been heavily involved in Scouting since he was a child and was also a proficient climber. This meant that he was very knowledgeable in the art of tying knots. Park had not denied this during his interviews with the police. He had told officers that he never discarded rope, cord or string as he was always able to make use of it.

Detectives presented Ide with the ropes and cords they had recovered from Park's home at Norland Avenue, along with others they found at Bluestones and Park's boat in 1997, the Mrs J. His keen forensic eye quickly identified examples of the exact same knots he had found on the packaging from Coniston Water: reef knots, bowlines, sheet-bends and figure-of-eights. There, too, were eye-splices and neatly-done heat sealed-ends of ropes.

The brilliance of Rodger Ide had provided detectives with compelling circumstantial evidence. It was clear Gordon Park had the knowledge and the wherewithal but the one thing Ide was unable to say conclusively was that the person who had tied the knots found at Bluestones was also the person who had tied those that trussed up Carol's body.

Police turned to another forensic scientist to examine the lead piping used to weigh down Carol's body. Like Rodger Ide, Philip Rydeard was an experienced expert in interpreting evidence and delivering devastating and irrefutable conclusions.

Four years earlier, at the 1993 trial of the two 10-year-old boys accused of murdering Liverpool toddler Jamie Bulger in a case that sickened the British public, Rydeard had matched a bruise on little Jamie's face with the shoe worn by Robert Thompson.

Rydeard was confronted by the flattened and folded piece of lead that had fallen out of the packaging around Carol's body. He unfolded it and discovered it was a length of 67 inches or 1.7 metres. The pipe bore a number of round indentations consistent with being flattened by a heavy implement, probably a hammer. These indentations were sharp suggesting to Rydeard that the flattening of the pipe had been done by a new or good-condition hammer. He believed the pipe could well be one from an overhead high-level cistern toilet system, common in period properties from the Victorian era predating the modern low-level-style cisterns. His deduction was confirmed by a Cumbrian plumber invited by police to inspect the pipe.

Rydeard also examined further lead piping and a toilet bowl that detectives had removed from Bluestones. He carefully inspected the characteristics and dimensions and established that it had a spigot at the back to accommodate a pipe consistent with an overhead cistern system. This spigot was the right diameter to fit the size of piping used to weigh down Carol's body. In interviews, detectives had been told by Park that he had never fitted an overhead high-level water cistern toilet when he built Bluestones. He admitted he had installed a new toilet system after Carol had disappeared.

Detectives were also keen for Philip Rydeard to inspect a series of hammers formerly belonging to Gordon Park which they had taken away from Bluestones shortly after the identification of Carol's body in late August. Meticulously, Rydeard tested each hammer, noting and recording the size and characteristics of the marks made by each implement. One of the hammers, a Stanley claw hammer, created an indentation similar in size to those he found on the lead piping from the body bag. He told detectives, however, that he could not say definitively that it was the same one used to flatten the pipe because it was a common hammer that had been in continuous production since 1978.

In their interviews with Park, detectives had been told that the hammers found at Bluestones were ones he had acquired in the years following 1976, most likely in the period of either his second or third marriages. Again, these were tantalising evidential conclusions for the detectives but not strong enough to damn Park with.

The nightdress that Carol's body was found in also proved a key piece of evidence. Even though dental records had successfully led to the identification of Carol, officers needed to pin-down the date of her death and the nightdress was important in this regard. Detectives were able to identify the dress when they showed photographs of it to the director of a mail order company called Halwins, which traded in the 1970s. The director was able to inform police that Carol's nightdress had been sold for a brief period in 1971.

Detectives knew this was an important piece of evidence. The fact that Carol's body was in the nightdress suggested she had been killed while wearing it and therefore was likely to have been at home at the time. This, too, would tie in with the theory that she died on or about the 17 July 1976, the day when Park took his children to Blackpool.

On 18 August, an expert using sonar equipment had plied up and down Coniston Water in a sailing boat between two buoys set 230 metres apart to provide impressions of the lake bed for the police.

Meanwhile, police divers returned to Coniston Water on Wednesday, 10 September and Tuesday, 30 September to make searches of the area close to where the body had been found. At a depth of 12 metres or so, they found various items of women's clothing dating from the 1970s, including footwear and a small red dress, and cosmetics also from the same era.

Also recovered was an unusual rock. The divers bagged up the various items of evidence.

The legal team representing Park asked Home Office pathologist Dr William Lawler to perform a fresh post mortem examination of the body on Thursday, 11 September.

Morale among detectives might have been bolstered by this circumstantial evidence but elsewhere enthusiasm for a successful prosecution of Gordon Park was muted.

Dick Binstead of the Crown Prosecution Service received a call to attend an important meeting in Newcastle with bosses who would decide whether to proceed or to pull the plug on legal proceedings against Park. Binstead was the Crown Prosecutor for Cumbria, which fell under the northern area of the CPS. It was his job to oversee the prosecution of criminal cases flowing through the county's courts. From day one of the Park investigation he had been involved in reviewing the evidence and in the preparation of case papers.

It was also his duty to convince his superiors this was a case that could be successfully prosecuted.

Gordon Park was behind bars at Preston Prison on remand; detectives and forensic experts were working around the clock in their efforts to find evidence that would stick. The second hearing at Barrow Magistrates Court was days away. And Binstead was now being summoned to a panel of top Crown Prosecutors. It wasn't encouraging and Binstead must have had a sinking feeling as he travelled across the moors of northern England to meet them.

He sat down in front of a panel of men headed by the Chief Crown Prosecutor. Rather than an enthusiastic welcome, Binstead was met with scepticism over the effectiveness of the evidence thus far. Binstead respected the views of the Chief Crown Prosecutor, who was a very experienced lawyer but he had reservations about the other men on the panel. One was a lawyer, admittedly, but one who had not been practically involved in case work for a long time. The third man was not a lawyer.

The meeting began and Binstead brought the panel up to speed on developments. The men listened but they did not share Binstead's belief that the case against Park was a strong one. No doubt frustrated, Binstead found it disturbing that the men had formed this view without actually reviewing the evidence for themselves first-hand. Binstead had given them no reason to reach this conclusion. It was as if they had already made up their minds. There was one glimmer of hope, however: their final decision would come once they had viewed the file of written evidence once it was ready and after they sought the views of the leading counsel in the case.

A dispirited Binstead shook the hands of the panel, collected his things and headed back to Cumbria. He believed the decision had already been made about the case in the minds of the Crown Prosecution Service.

Naturally, Det Supt Ian Douglas and his team of detectives

were disappointed by Binstead's report of the meeting. Binstead sensed there was a feeling, if unspoken, that the police had anticipated the CPS's unenthusiastic response. In his memoir about the case, Binstead later wrote, "We resolved to present the case in the best light we could in an attempt to convert the 'doubters'."

The detectives also agreed to Binstead's intention to remove Crown objections to Park being granted bail at the next court hearing on Tuesday, 9 September.

20

Brains Trust

As the lights went out in his cell on that first night of his remand, Gordon Park wondered what would become of him. Prison life was so alien to him, so far removed from the life he was used to living. His life was about freedom, wide open spaces, lakes and mountains; now he was staring at four walls, trapped within a box. It was a world he did not understand, a world he was not prepared for, a world that petrified him. His legal team instructed him to be guarded in the presence of other inmates or the prison officers, to be suspicious of their motives. Alarmingly, Park was told he could be a target to other prisoners who might want to attack him. With these terrifying thoughts in his head, Park was taken first to the hospital in Preston Prison, where he spent four days acclimatising to this new world. Then he was transferred to F Ward, where the most vulnerable prisoners were held.

And so he lay at night in the darkness, struggling with the turn of events.

The days were long, locked away. The highlight was the mail

that arrived, letters that might lift his spirits. One day he was reading one written by his stepson Stuart when he became overcome with emotion and broke down crying. Another prisoner called Steve with whom he had become friendly sat with him, offered silent reassurance before asking Park if he was all right. Park looked at Steve, his face smeared in tears. Steve reassured Park everything would be OK. The show of compassion from the other prisoner touched Park and he never forgot this unexpected touch of humanity.

A week after his first court appearance, Park was brought for a second hearing at Barrow Magistrates Court on Tuesday, 9 September. Once more a crowd assembled outside. He was brought into the dock by security guards, watched by the public gallery, reporters with pens poised, and his solicitor Barbara Forrester and Crown Prosecutor Philip Bates.

Bates raised no objection to a bail application after a set of appropriate conditions were agreed. These conditions were that Park should hand in his passport, should live in Higher Green, Astley, in Tyldesley in Manchester with his sister and not try to contact any of the 11 named prosecution witnesses, who included his children, Vanessa, Jeremy and Rachael, his second wife Cath Sillars, guest house owners Anne and Derrick Walker, David Brearley and close friends from the past. He was to observe a curfew between 9pm and 8am and was instructed to present himself twice a week, on Tuesdays and Fridays between 9am and noon, at Tyldesley police station in Greater Manchester. A map of Cumbria was shown to magistrates marked with the area covering Furness and Coniston. Conditions of Park's bail were that he must not enter this designated area unless it was to appear in court or for a pre-arranged meeting with his legal team.

Prosecutor Bates told magistrates these were "unusual but not exceptional" requirements. The date for the next court hearing was set for Tuesday, 18 November.

Gordon Park walked free from the court with a series of complex restraints upon his liberty.

At the end of October, Det Supt Ian Douglas's detectives delivered a file outlining all the evidence to Dick Binstead and the Crown Prosecution Service. This was the sum total of the blood, sweat and toil of officers such as DC Doug Marshall and his dedicated colleagues. The hopes of convicting Gordon Park and of seeing justice not only for Carol but also for Ivor Price and the wider family rested on this complex and vital collection of papers.

Binstead knew the contents needed to be reviewed very carefully if the senior Crown Prosecution Service team were to be convinced. He acknowledged the need for a "brains trust" to comb through the evidence, so he brought in two experienced experts: a special casework lawyer and another Crown Prosecutor from Barrow. Collectively, they had more than 50 years of experience. "Though I say it myself," he later wrote, "this was the best possible collection of minds available in Cumbria to weigh up and assess the evidence in this case."

Binstead sent the file to each of them for review before they spent a full day talking at length, highlighting the case's strengths but also sketching out the weak spots, for it would be these upon which the whole case's success could hinge.

They discovered there were a number of weak areas that would be exploited by Park's defence lawyers should the case go to trial. For example, there was the question of the time-frame of Carol's murder. If it were true she had been killed on Saturday, 17 July 1976, the day Park took the children to Blackpool, when and how had he found time to murder her, truss up the body and dispose of it in Coniston Water? How had he accomplished this before rigor mortis set in and without the children's knowledge? Had he left Vanessa, Jeremy and Rachael alone at Bluestones during his trip to Coniston, if indeed that is what he had done? How had this been achieved without his leaving traces of a brutal murder?

They were also concerned about the time that had elapsed since Carol had gone missing. Twenty-one years. That was a very long time, a fact that could undermine the prosecution's case and no doubt one that would be exploited to the full by Park's legal team. Frustratingly, the statement Park had given to police in 1976 about the events of that summer had gone missing along with Carol's missing person's file.

Another significant worry was the number of other men who might have had motives to kill Carol, including former lovers and the man who had murdered her sister, John Rapson.

By the end of that long October day all three men were convinced there was sufficient evidence for a realistic prospect of a conviction. As they finished their discussions and put on their coats, they agreed the case should proceed to trial.

All that remained now was to convince the heads of the Crown Prosecution Service in Newcastle.

21

No Stone Left
Unturned

Park was now living at his sister's address in Manchester. The police kept a close eye on him to ensure he observed the 9pm to 8am curfew. Park found this annoying as it kept him from his early morning run.

The condition also meant he was separated from Jenny, who stayed in Barrow due to work commitments and to look after Jane and Stuart. Park was not allowed to make contact with his own children as they were to be called as witnesses by the Crown Prosecution Service.

As the preliminary court hearings continued, however, Park's bail conditions were relaxed in late 1997. He was allowed to see his family once more and they booked a cottage in the Lake District to spend a quiet Christmas together.

Following the day-long review with the two legal experts, Dick Binstead had sent the file of evidence to the chief Crown Prosecutor at Newcastle with a strident covering note outlining his views and those of the police. There was nothing more he could do. He waited for a response.

For weeks there was silence. Then one day towards the end of November Binstead got his answer. He received a reply from the Chief Crown Prosecutor containing a copy of his own review of the evidence. Binstead read the document carefully, hopeful that there was a positive outcome.

The Chief Crown Prosecutor concluded: based on the evidence in his opinion there was not a realistic prospect of a conviction. Binstead blinked, processing what he had read. The document had identified the same weak spots in the evidence that had concerned Binstead and his "brains trust".

Binstead and his colleagues believed these weaknesses could be countered by the weight of circumstantial evidence. It appeared, however, CPS bosses were concerned there was no "smoking gun", no scientific evidence linking Gordon Park directly to the murder. Binstead was disappointed. If Park hadn't killed Carol, based on all that incriminating detail, who had?

Binstead's last hope now was for an independent leading counsel, or senior barrister, to review the evidence and give his or her opinion. Binstead hoped this leading barrister might be Brian Leveson, who had successfully prosecuted Rosemary West in 1995. West and her husband Fred were the notorious serial killers from Gloucester in a case that became known as the 'house of horrors'. In 2011, Brian Leveson would head the high-profile Government public inquiry into the "culture, practices and ethics" of the British press amid scandalous allegations of phone hacking by *News of the World* reporters. Disappointingly for Binstead, Leveson wasn't available. Instead, the task fell to a Manchester barrister, Jack Price. Binstead didn't know him. Nevertheless, he prepared a brief for Price and on 19 December he travelled to Manchester for a meeting in Price's chambers. Binstead was accompanied by one of the members of his "brains trust" and they were joined by the deputy of the CPS panel in Newcastle and senior detectives from Cumbria Police. The meeting was not a positive one for Binstead and the detectives. They came out of the meeting dejected: the months of hard work had not been enough.

The task fell to Dick Binstead to issue the formal notice informing Gordon Park that all charges against him were to be dropped.

Park's solicitor Barbara Forrester received a phone call from the Crown Prosecution Service. She was told the case against her client was being "discontinued" due to insufficient evidence. It was all out of the blue and the call was over and done with very quickly. Forrester was rather taken aback and had to process the information before she called Park. It might have been unexpected but it was something she had advised Park could happen given the length of time since Carol's disappearance.

Park was still living at his sister's home in Manchester under the conditions of his bail. Forrester lifted the phone, dialled the number of Park's sister and told him she had some good news. Park was shocked and could barely take in this new information. This news put him in the clear. Park was relieved and happy. Forrester kept the call brief and left him to reflect on his good fortune.

But she knew reality would soon settle on her client. With the police's commitment to continue investigating, there was a real possibility Park could be re-charged if circumstances changed.

As the news sank in, she prepared what she was going to say to the press.

Deborah Kermode reported on this latest development for that week's *Westmorland Gazette*. The story ran on page one with the headline: "'Lady in lake' murder charge is dropped". She wrote that Park was "shocked and happy". She had stood with other reporters as a statement from Park was released through Barbara Forrester.

Park, the statement read, was "most relieved" by the news and wished to thank his family for their "love and support" through what had been a "most difficult" time. He also expressed gratitude for the help from his friends and the messages from "well-wishers".

"I would now like to put all this – including the events of 21 years ago – behind me, and return to my everyday life," Park said via the statement. "In order to do this, I request that the press and media respect not only my privacy but also that of my family."

Barbara Forrester had then spoken directly to reporters. She described Park's reaction and mood following the news: "He was stunned, very shocked, very relieved and very happy to hear the news." She added, "Mr Park has always maintained that he was not guilty of the charge, and that he had nothing to do with Carol Ann Park's disappearance."

She told reporters that Park had no immediate plans to return to Cumbria from his sister's home. She repeated Park's request to the media: "He and his family would be grateful if they could be given the time and privacy to return to their everyday lives."

Reporters asked whether Park would be seeking compensation from the police over his arrest. Forrester replied that the question of compensation had not yet been discussed by Park and his legal team.

In her story, Deborah had asked the Crown Prosecution Service's press officer on why the decision had been taken to drop charges against Park. "This was not a decision which was taken lightly at all," said Barbara Flint of the CPS. "There was close consultation and liaison with the police at every stage, and believe me, no stone was left unturned."

The very public manner in which this turn of events played out must have irritated and frustrated detectives such as Doug Marshall. He and the other investigators could do nothing but watch their boss Det Supt Ian Douglas make the same sounds of optimism that Carol's murderer would be brought to justice. DS Douglas told the press the case had not been closed and police would "continue to actively investigate the murder". But the note of optimism might have sounded increasingly hollow when Douglas said, "The force has put in a lot of effort on this inquiry and a lot of good work has been done. However, our job is made all the more difficult by the fact that it is more than 21 years since Carol Ann Park was murdered."

It sounded more like defeat than a lead-from-the-front rallying cry.

The words of the CPS that "no stone was left unturned" would take on an ironic new meaning six years later when the chickens finally came home to roost for Gordon Park.

Chapter 22: A Herculean Effort

The news reverberated around the world. Headlines from the United States to Australia illustrated the global interest in the Lady in the Lake case. It was like something from a classic detective novel by Agatha Christie or the hugely popular *Inspector*

Morse television series of the time. There was something very English about the story: the respectable middle-class school-teacher accused of brutally killing his wife and dropping her into a picture-postcard lake. It was the sort of scenario George Orwell outlined in his classic essay *Decline of the English Murder*. In it, Orwell examines the public's fascination with murders they read about after Sunday lunch in the *News of the World*. Usually these murders were committed by middle-class men in respectable jobs, set against a domestic background. Orwell was satirising tabloid newspapers' obsession with real murder cases for commercial gain. But he was also targeting us, the common reader, whose taste for such stories was programmed deep in our DNA, an impulse as primal as our instinct to survive.

Park's friends and acquaintances welcomed news of the CPS decision. "I'm just glad his ordeal is over," a neighbour on Norland Avenue told reporters. Another acquaintance, Colin Lander, one of Park's friends from Roa Island Boating Club, said, "Good luck to the lad. If the police haven't got enough evidence, who else is to say what happened?"

Support for Park also came from an unexpected quarter. One of his former pupils at South Newbarns School stepped forward and told reporters of how Park had been the best teacher who taught her. Ruth Niven, now aged 30 and living in Kendal, remembered Park as a very popular and friendly teacher. Speaking to a reporter from the *Evening Mail*, she said, "I really liked him. He was probably the best teacher I ever had. I thought he was absolutely fantastic. A really nice bloke. He was very well-liked among all my friends."

Niven was a pupil at South Newbarns in 1976 at the time of Carol's disappearance and was a contemporary of Park's own children at the school. She recalled reading a newspaper report when Carol vanished and the outpouring of sympathy for Park who was left to raise his family single-handedly. Nobody at the time suspected Park might be connected to the disappearance. "As an adult I often used to see him around Barrow," Niven told the reporter. "He always stopped and spoke to me. When I heard he had been arrested I couldn't believe it. I just thought 'no way'."

But for Ivor Price and his family, the news was devastating. Ivor was stunned and for the first time in many months he had very little to say to reporters. This was a terrible new blow to a man who had lived a life of battery at the hands of fate. Speaking at his home at Lord Roberts Street in Walney, Ivor said, "My main concern at this time is my family. I am not prepared to comment at this stage. I just hope Cumbria Police will continue to pursue the matter in bringing to justice whoever is guilty."

Gordon Park might have desired privacy but, as he would discover, there was too much public interest in the case for his wish to be granted. And in due course, he would use the power of the press in an effort to rehabilitate his reputation with the public.

Cumbria Police were devastated. After the hours and hours of toil it was awful, dispiriting news for the detectives. DC Doug Marshall had interviewed Park and formally charged him. He was especially despondent after Park was released. "There was obviously a strong circumstantial case building," he recalled, "and there was always an expectation that there might have been some forensic material that might have come in that never did."

The police were left with a dilemma. Gordon Park was the

man they believed murdered Carol Park but their evidence had not been enough to bring him to trial. The police budget was not infinite. A stark decision had to be taken. Marshall recalled, "Mike Warner, who was the DS, and I were given a brief: you've got basically six months to go out and find whatever evidence there is and then it'll get shut down."

Marshall and Warner knew they had to work quickly and efficiently. Six months was not long. They spent time looking at what evidence they did have: the lead pipe, the ropes, the baby doll night dress. Was there crucial evidence hidden within these macabre objects?

"Mike and I were travelling all over the country," Marshall recalled, "speaking to people about clothing, the lead piping, ropes, everything. And much good work was done during those six months."

By the summer of 1998 they knew their time was nearly up. The two detectives were tireless in their pursuit of their goal. "I don't remember being at home," Marshall remembered. "I was on the road, literally weekly, going up and down the country, seeing folk, and going to places to check clothing, checking labels, checking where things could have come from, retracing all the steps."

The deadline arrived. There was no more they could do. Was it enough? They had to pull together what they had, the culmination of half a year of Herculean effort. It was time to present their work to the police top brass.

But when the detectives went to see their bosses it was not good news.

"The bosses decided there wasn't enough to get him [Park] back in or to recharge him or to carry on with the case," remembered Marshall, his voice sounding a note of disappointment even after all these years.

And so Gordon Park remained a free man, his protests of innocence still untested in a court of law. For the police, the case had become an insurmountable brick wall. The case remained open and other possible suspects were explored such as David Brearley and John Rapson. But Gordon Park remained their chief person of interest.

22

Putting the Record Straight

Park's family were exhilarated by his release from the murder charge. It came after months of intense pressure and at the point where Jenny and his children were preparing for the ordeal of a trial. But this sense of relief would be short lived.

The spectre of the murder charge might have been lifted but it was not the same as an acquittal by a jury. The intense media coverage had tainted Park in the eyes of the public. Whether it was spoken or not, there was a lingering suspicion, a sense of there being no smoke without fire. The Park family felt he had been demonised by the media. Privately, Park was furious. The family became suspicious of every call, believing that their phone might be tapped.

The media and the public's fascination, however, would never diminish, whatever Park and his family thought. In the coming months there would be a Channel 4 television documentary called *The Ladies of the Lake* which examined murder cases where female victims had been disposed of in watery graves. It featured the previously-mentioned case of airline pilot Peter Hogg, who had murdered his wife in October 1976 – eerily, only months after Carol Park's disappearance – and had dumped her body in Wast Water before it was discovered in March 1984 by divers searching for a missing student from France. Hogg was found guilty of manslaughter and was jailed but was released after 15 months. Inevitably, the programme featured the disappearance of Carol Park. Unlike the Hogg case, there was no guilty perpetrator identified as Park had been released.

Everywhere he went, Park would feel eyes on him. People stared at him when he was browsing in B&Q, his favourite DIY store. He wondered if he would ever put the case behind him.

Seeing the dilemma, solicitor Barbara Forrester told Park there was something he could do to satisfy the media once and for all and silence the gossip mongers. She advised Park and Jenny to give one exclusive interview to a newspaper.

Readers of the *Mail on Sunday* opened their copies on 18 January 1998 to see a photograph of Park in glasses, a white shirt and grey jumper underneath a tan leather jacket. He was staring wistfully across Ullswater in the Lake District.

"The last time I saw Carol was a Saturday morning in the summer of 1976," Park told reporter Laurie Mansbridge.

"It was not the first time she had left," Park said. "She had walked out on me about six times already, sometimes returning the next day, other times leaving me for months on end for other men."

Carol had left no note, just her wedding and engagement rings abandoned on her dressing table which Park took as an indication their marriage was over. "It was 'wait and see' time again," Park said.

It was a long news feature, running to 3,000 words and in it Park poured out his heart. The reporter wrote, "So began one of the most intriguing unsolved murder mysteries of our times: Who killed the lady in the lake? The man speaking is 53-year-old Gordon Park and it is 10 days since the charge that he murdered his wife Carol more than 21 years ago was sensationally dropped."

Mansbridge offered the basic outline of the case since Carol's body was discovered five months earlier and then brought readers up to speed on what had happened to Park since the murder charge had been dropped: he had initially gone into hiding with wife Jenny to avoid hounding by the press. In a dramatic tabloid drumroll, readers were informed, "But now he has broken his silence in an exclusive interview with the *Mail on Sunday*, in which he says 'I did not kill Carol – and I want people to know the truth'."

In words that must have upset and unsettled Ivor Price, Park said, "I want to put the record straight and draw a line under these terrible events… I want her murderer caught. After all I've been through, the police owe it to me."

The article made it clear Park believed Carol might have been murdered by one of her lovers. He theorised that this unknown man turned up at Bluestones and took her away when she walked out on their marriage. Park had an explanation for why he failed to report her missing for six weeks: it was because she had left him before. He had waited for her to return. He said he had not been unduly concerned as Carol was "young, attractive, vivacious and quite capable of looking after herself". It was only when she didn't come back that he alerted the authorities. They were initially suspicious of him because of the delay in contacting the authorities, he said. Senior detectives questioned him and the police investigated the mystery for six months in 1976. They checked inside his freezer, the loft at Bluestones and asked questions about what Carol took with her while the children were asked whether she had said goodbye to them.

His recollection of the efforts to find her were thus, "We used the media and the Salvation Army to try to find her. The police made inquiries." He said there was a report of a car seen outside Bluestones on the day she went missing and Gordon attributed this to Carol having gone off with a man. There were reported sightings of her, too.

Park tried to tug at readers' emotions. He couldn't grasp why Carol had walked out on him and three "lovely" children. "It is very hard when three little children ask why Mummy has not come home or when she is returning," he said. He painted himself as happy in the marriage, it excited him, along with running their home and looking after the children. Carol, he claimed, wanted more than him and came alive only when they were in company. It never occurred to him he was holding her back, but with hindsight he could see this must have been what she thought.

He believed their marriage crumbled under the pressure of having three children under the age of three. They had little money, rarely went out together and Carol was triggered into crying over minor things. "I still look at the photos of the happy times together," he told the journalist, "but ask myself: if she'd loved us, how could she leave us?"

The details of Carol's affairs with other men and the battle for custody of the children were picked over. "There was no time for self-pity," he said. "My primary responsibility was to carry on working in order to look after the children." His existence had alternated between working and sleeping. He had become an "emotional cripple" but had no choice but to keep going. He had not burdened the children with knowledge of their mother's affairs. He wanted them to retain a positive picture of her.

"The notion that she was dead just never entered my head," he said. "The police did not say that they suspected me of murder, but they pointed out that if ever a body was found, I would be the first suspect."

Park was keen to dispel the media's negative characterisation of him in the days after the discovery of Carol's body when he was on holiday. "It was the start of a nightmare," he recalled. "The media wrongly reported that we were in hiding and that the police were in France looking for us. In fact, it just took us two days to get home."

Park said he answered the police's questions as fully and honestly as he could and had believed detectives would release him once they realised their mistake. Therefore it had been chilling to be formally charged with Carol's murder and he had found himself on remand at Preston Prison. "From the warmth of France, I suddenly found myself alongside murderers and rapists," he said. He had been terrified. Support had come from the most unexpected of quarters: the lifers in the prison.

Park made it clear he could not have survived the previous months without the love and support of Jenny, his wife. He said he did not want to "sound smug" but he and Jenny were "totally happy together, beyond anyone's possible understanding".

The reporter had interviewed Jenny and asked what her husband was like. "Gordon is so caring and compassionate, gentle, loving – and he listens," she replied. "I'm horrified to think anyone could suspect he was capable of murder."

In the final part of the interview, Park talked about the punishing police interviews, which had begun in a civilised manner but became increasingly aggressive. He claimed his solicitor had to stop the interview on three occasions. Detectives refused to believe what he was telling them, he claimed, and he thought they were trying to break him down. "I knew they could have no direct evidence linking me to this crime because there isn't any," he said. "I did not do it." His biggest fear, though, had been that a "slick-tongued barrister" might convince a jury of his guilt. "How do you prove you did not do something?" he protested.

The police were continuing their investigation, he said, something he welcomed because an answer of what truly happened would allow him to clear his name. He knew members of the public would doubt his innocence and that was why he was keen for police to identify the true killer.

The interview moved into the final section. Park said Coniston Water had always been a favourite place and held many happy memories. He had sailed there frequently in his youth and also in the years after Carol disappeared. But since the discovery of her body he hadn't returned.

Reporter Mansbridge signed off the newspaper feature thus, "A thought crosses his mind and brings tears to his eyes. 'I must have sailed over her body dozens of times,' he muses. 'I cannot see that I will ever enjoy the place again.'"

Gordon Park was paid £50,000 for this interview.

The newspaper article and Park's taunting of the police had been a tour de force. But it did not surprise detectives at Cumbria CID. "I think this behaviour was something that was quite expected of him," detective Doug Marshall remembered. "He was definitely a man that liked to control things. And I think this was a further ploy of his to try and control the situation that he had found himself in. He was someone we thought had murdered his wife and that justice should be done."

Park's peacocking did not concern the detectives.

23

The Inquest

In the summer of 1998 the news agenda moved on as it always does. The headlines were dominated by the sex scandal of US President Bill Clinton and White House intern Monica Lewinsky. On holiday that August I sat on the beach at Tenby in Pembrokeshire reading the sordid details. For the time being I had pushed the Lady in the Lake case out of my thoughts. When I returned to work at the start of September, though, the spectre of the case loomed once more and I was assigned to cover it. There was a new Editor in charge at the *Gazette*. John Lannaghan had retired and Mike Glover, a former editor of the *Bradford Telegraph and Argus*, was appointed as his successor.

The inquest was set for Monday, 7 September. I made an early start from Lancaster and drove directly to Barrow-in-Furness. I made my way along Abbey Road and slotted my car into a space on Market Street car park to the rear of the Town Hall. I had seen the building many times before on visits to the town as a child and during reporting trips. But now as I walked towards it, the sound of seagulls circling overhead, I could see what an impressive, imposing structure the town hall was in the early September sunlight. Building work had begun in 1877 and the finished snecked red sandstone edifice was in the Gothic Revival style. It was a wide-facing building with graduated slate roofs and an impressive clock tower rising like a NASA space rocket ready for take-off. I walked around the edge of the building; people were milling around the town hall's arched entrance on Duke Street. I knew there would be huge media interest in the inquest because Gordon Park was due to give evidence. There were numerous TV news teams arranged around cameras on tripods. There were reporters in suits and smart clothes.

I decided to go straight inside. I knew Gordon Park was likely to arrive as late as possible to limit press attention. I was also keen to get a good seat in the inquest room.

It was only much later I learned that the Town Hall was where Ivor and Maureen Price had seen Carol during a children's show 10 days before her disappearance. It was also where Carol worked as a 17-year-old clerk when she first met Gordon Park.

I walked into the large entrance hall and to the right was a broad stone staircase with an ornate balustrade leading to a half-landing. I climbed the steps to the upper floor where more people were conversing. I assumed they were witnesses, legal figures and more journalists. The inquest was to be held in the large council chamber, high ceilinged with wood panelling and ornate decoration. It was already filling up. I recognised some of the people as journalists by their notebooks and pens. Others I took to be friends and family of the Parks and the Prices. I quickly found a seat facing the coroner's chair.

Overseeing the inquest would be Her Majesty's Coroner Ian

Smith, who was responsible for Furness and South Cumbria. I had reported on a number of his inquest hearings over the years. He had a reputation for speaking out on matters arising from hearings that he felt had wider pressing social importance. I was keen to see how he would respond in this case.

An inquest is not a criminal court. There is no apportioning of blame, it is purely to establish how somebody died and in what circumstances. We knew in advance that Park would be under instruction from his solicitor not to say anything incriminating that could later be used in a criminal investigation. That, of course, would be Park's right.

Now more people streamed into the room as the start time approached. Ian Smith arrived with his colleague Charlie Johnson. Ivor Price, dressed in a dark suit, crisp white shirt and striped tie, walked in with his wife Maureen and two daughters, Kay and Claire. Ivor greeted Ian Smith respectfully and formally, "Good morning, Mr Coroner."

Like everyone else in the room, I waited for the arrival of Gordon Park and for the inquest to begin.

Outside the town hall anticipation was rising for Park's appearance. Journalists and TV camera crews leapt into action when a brown saloon car pulled up. Two burly men in suits emerged, followed by a blank-faced Park, who was wearing a black suit, white shirt and dark patterned tie. He was holding a thick paperback book in his hand. The men, from private investigation firm Astute Paralegal Group in Kendal, linked arms with Park and quickly rushed him past the whirring cameras into the town hall. It was a bizarre scene that would be watched later by millions of TV viewers. It was a public relations disaster because Park looked like a guilty man being escorted like a prisoner.

There was a hush as Park and his two escorts entered the inquest room. All eyes burned into him. He took his seat on the front row to the left of the coroner.

The hearing was due to begin at 10am but coroner Ian Smith announced there would be a delay as Home Office pathologist Dr Edmund Tapp was snarled up in traffic due to an accident on the A590 through South Cumbria. Once Tapp arrived, Smith asked him to present the findings of his post-mortem examination of Carol Park's remains. Tapp was the first of seven witnesses who would give evidence that day.

Dr Tapp revealed there were a number of breaks in Carol's jaw and other facial injuries. He believed these had been caused by blows from a heavy, sharp object. The impact to the face seemed to have been caused deliberately with a focus on the central part of the face.

It was grim listening. The room was completely silent. My pen scratched shorthand symbols quickly across my notebook. I looked up and consciously studied Gordon Park to see his reaction but he sat impassively, his thoughts inscrutable. I'm sure I was not the only one observing him during Dr Tapp's evidence.

Carol's body, Tapp said, had been contained in what he originally thought was a canvas drawstring bag but then he had realised it was actually a pinafore dress drawn tight with a string. He described the awful moment teeth and parts of the facial bones fell out of another bag inside. The remains were in a badly decomposed state. The blue nylon rope binding Carol's body into a foetal position had been tied and knotted in an "extremely complex manner". For the body to have been manipulated into such a position, Dr Tapp said, it must have been extremely flexible.

He talked about the damage to the hands, consistent with injuries one might sustain trying to defend oneself. He concluded by saying he believed the fatal injuries had been caused by shattering blows from "an axe or heavy chopper".

An independent consultant pathologist under the instructions of Gordon Park's legal team had examined the remains and now gave evidence. Dr William Lawler disputed Dr Tapp's view that the injuries had been caused by such an implement. Lawler said the precise cause of death could not be ascertained beyond reasonable doubt given the length of time the body had lain at the bottom of Coniston Water.

As the morning went on, the coroner called on further witnesses to give evidence. David Mason was one of two Kendal divers who spoke. He described the heartstopping moment he and dive colleagues discovered the package in Coniston and realised it was a body. Det Sgt Michael Warner of Barrow Police outlined the timeline of the police investigation. He spoke of the knots that had been used to secure the body and said they had been tied by someone with significant mountaineering or climbing experience. He told the hearing that Carol Park had been photographed at Christmas the year before her disappearance wearing the pinafore dress that had been used as a shroud for her body. Gordon Park listened without reaction to the detective's words. DS Warner told the hearing of Carol's two affairs during her marriage and her time living in Middlesbrough.

Smith then called for Ivor Price to speak as a witness. Speaking slowly and with emotion in his voice, his wife and daughters beside him, Ivor talked about his sister's early life and her infectious life-affirming personality. He revealed she had told him of her deep unhappiness over her marriage two days before she went missing.

Then it was the moment everyone had waited for. Coroner Ian Smith said he would take the evidence of Gordon Park. There was coughing and shuffling of feet from the gallery. Park sat like a statue. He stared straight ahead, clearly uncomfortable under scrutiny. Smith said he would ask questions of Park and would allow further questions from Ivor Price and Park's solicitor Barbara Forrester, whom Smith had permitted to sit alongside Park to provide counsel.

And so the coroner began his questions.

Smith asked him about the state of his marriage after 1974.

Park did not answer.

Smith asked whether he was unhappy about his wife's conduct.

Park did not answer.

Had she moved out of the marital home and if so, how often?

Park gave no answer.

Each time, Smith's questions hung in the air like unseen distress flares.

The only sound was of pens scratching furiously on paper. There was an awkward tension and I scanned the room; everyone was gripped.

Smith asked Park why he had put up with his wife's affairs and her abandonment of the marital home.

Now Park felt he was able to speak.

When he did so it was often in a whisper.

"I loved my wife," he said. "She was the mother of my children. We had a really good family. I believed we could make it right."

He spoke about the trip to Blackpool, the day of her disappearance, "She decided she didn't wish to go. I can't remember the reason why but it wasn't significant then. Neither was her sudden change of mind."

Smith asked, "How did you feel about looking after the children?"

"That was what was to be done so I did it," Park said. "The children knew they were going somewhere special." He said the children would have been disappointed had they not gone.

This was the first occasion Park had spoken in public about the events of that day. He told the inquest that when they left Bluestones on Saturday, 17 January 1976, Carol was alive and well in her bed. He could not recall whether the children had seen her before they left but it was not unusual for them to not see her.

Smith asked Park what his reaction was to Carol's disappearance and the discovery of her rings on her bedroom dressing table.

Betraying no emotion, Park replied in a cool manner that was clipped and slightly sharp, "Shall I answer this sensibly if at all? I was disappointed. This was not something new to me. I thought 'here we go again'."

It was a jarring moment.

Ivor Price was invited to put his questions to Park. He asked whether Carol had been ill on that fateful morning in 1976. Responding directly to his former brother-in-law, Park spoke in a louder voice, "Ivor, I don't know why she didn't come. She had worked the day before. If I could tell you what she said I would do so. But the reason then wasn't significant. It has become significant but it wasn't significant then."

Ivor asked why Park had left it six weeks to report her missing.

"I was waiting for her," Park replied. "It was very simple. I expected her to make some contact."

This was the first public interaction between Park and Ivor Price since Carol's body had been discovered just over a year earlier. It was electric, heavy with unarticulated emotion.

The inquest took a short break. It was an intense hearing and much of the evidence was difficult to listen to. As an observer, reporting on the hearing, it was hard to imagine how Ivor Price and his family were feeling.

The room emptied as members of the public and journalists vacated to stretch their legs and get some fresh air. The area outside the inquest room, encircling the main staircase, was abuzz. I found myself talking with other journalists, including, I recall, Richard Wells of the BBC. All we could talk about, naturally, was Gordon Park. We'd thought the same thing: would he betray guilt or otherwise? And of course now that we'd seen him in the flesh, we were none the wiser. He certainly came across as a cold, unemotional man. But would any of us have reacted differently under such scrutiny? The consensus was that Park, who had sat with his paperback, was a book that could not be judged by its cover.

We were called back to the hearing; the coroner was about to reconvene the inquest.

It was now time for Ian Smith to record his verdict. He took his seat, the room silent, save for the sound of papers being shuffled and coughs from the gallery.

Many of the reporters, particularly those from the national press, were unfamiliar with Ian Smith. I knew what to expect and he did not disappoint.

"This case, this killing, has attracted the name throughout the media of 'The Lady in the Lake'," he began, "and I have to say that gives a certain romanticism almost to what is most certainly not in any sense romantic."

He continued, "This lady was killed, brutally and horribly, her body was to some extent mutilated, thrown into Coniston and I can see why the media have made of it what they have but I ask them not to lose sight of the fact that this was an extremely vicious and an extremely brutal murder of this woman."

My pen skittered across my notebook. Around me I could hear the press pack frantically scribbling too.

Smith said, "I believe she was killed on or about July 17. I find it inconceivable that this lady would have gone away and just abandoned her children completely."

Based on the evidence, he said, he was making no indication of who had killed her, adding, "And I don't want anyone to go out of here and to say, or infer, that I did that. There is no evidence that she died at Bluestones. I don't know where she died."

Smith never usually prepared his summings-up in writing, preferring to speak naturally in the moment, guided by detailed notes and trusting in his instinct. And his instinct on this September day was to send a message to her killer, and this is what he said, "As regards who did it, I hope that if that person is still alive, which 20 odd years later they may not be, if that person is still alive, then I hope they have a conscience and I hope that their conscience is troubling them."

There was complete silence in the room at that moment.

I glanced up at Park. I wanted to see his face, to see if there was a reaction, even the slightest. But there was none. He sat stony faced, motionless, and emotionless. I noted that Smith did not look at Park when he spoke that final rhetorical statement to Carol's killer, and he carefully chose the pronoun 'they' rather than 'he'. Twenty-odd years later Smith noted in his memoirs *More Deaths Than One* that he consciously stared straight ahead at that moment.

Smith recorded a verdict of unlawful killing.

Before the inquest concluded, the question of what should now become of Carol Park's earthly remains was raised and it would become a source of conflict.

24

A Mother's Remains

As the long, emotional inquest drew to a close, coroner Ian Smith told the families and the police, "I think after all this time a line needs to be drawn."

The remains of Carol Park had been examined and re-examined by experts. It was time for those earthly remains to be laid to rest. This was certainly the view of Carol's children. Solicitor Peter Sharp – whom I knew from reporting the magistrates courts in Kendal and South Lakeland – spoke on behalf of Vanessa, Jeremy and Rachael. He told the inquest the children supported their father fully and were now requesting the release of their mother's body. Speaking firmly, Sharp explained that it was the family's intention to have their mother's remains cremated.

This request was vehemently opposed from two quarters: the police and Ivor Price.

Det Supt Ian Douglas said that if anyone were to be arrested subsequently on suspicion of murdering Carol Park then that person might want the remains examined by an independent pathologist. He believed this would be right and proper.

"We would prefer to retain the remaining body parts in the interests of justice," he told the coroner. He conceded, though, that should Mr Smith be mindful of releasing the remains, then as a concession he would prefer that the body be buried rather than cremated.

Ivor Price offered his views on the matter. He, too, was opposed to cremation of his sister's remains. "I would prefer them to be buried in case there is ever a need for them to be re-examined," he said. "I said last year I would have liked her to be buried with my parents and sister, Christine, who are all in one grave at a cemetery in Barrow. But I do have every sympathy with the Park children and I feel they should have the mortal remains laid to rest."

Coroner Ian Smith sat quietly, processing the requests. He told the hearing, "My decision is that the body parts should be returned to the family."

It was over. It had been emotionally draining, electric in places, and incredibly sad.

The inquest room emptied, like gas escaping from a balloon. I closed my notebook, capped my pen and quickly made my way down the stairs with the other reporters. We had the inquest preserved in ink but now we needed the reaction.

Ivor Price and his wife and daughters had found it overwhelming. When I asked Ivor for a comment, he politely declined other than saying, "It's a difficult time."

The reaction we all wanted, of course, was Gordon Park's. But we knew it was highly unlikely he would hang around to speak to reporters. Predictably, he was whisked away by the two private investigators in another misjudged moment that did nothing to improve the public's perception of him.

Solicitor Barbara Forrester released a prepared statement from Park to reporters. In it, Park said, "I am pleased that the ordeal for my family has come to an end. The past 12 months have been a great strain on all of us, particularly my children, who have had to come to terms, not only with the now certainty that their mother is dead but also with the pressures on me during this time." He thanked Vanessa, Jeremy and Rachael and his wife Jenny for their support.

Park's statement concluded with an appeal, "I hope that the media and the public will now allow us the privacy to rebuild and then continue our lives."

TV journalists scribbled final notes and delivered their reports to camera, while the national print reporters went off to file their stories. I wasn't under the same immediate pressure: the *Gazette* did not go to press for another three days, one of the drawbacks of being a weekly paper.

I began composing the opening to my story as I returned to my car where I'd left it in the shadow of Barrow Town Hall. I looked up at the imposing clock tower, climbed behind the wheel and set off for home. The words tumbled out at my computer the next day. My report was published that Friday with the headline: 'Husband pleads to be left alone: 'Lady in lake' unlawfully killed – inquest.' The sub-editors had used a photograph of Gordon Park's arrival at Barrow Town Hall taken from the BBC's television report, with the caption: 'I loved my wife – GORDON PARK'. There were photographs of Ivor Price and Dr Edmund Tapp.

My story began: 'The husband of 'lady in the lake' Carol Ann Park this week pleaded to be left alone to rebuild his life after an inquest into her death recorded a verdict of unlawful killing.' I gave readers a full account of the inquest and the evidence that was heard, along with the statement from Park read out by his legal team.

The following day, Wednesday, 9 September, I turned 30. When I walked into the *Gazette* office there were red and blue and yellow balloons tacked to the wall next to my desk and streamers dangling down onto my desk. Steve Barber, one of the *Gazette*'s photographers, snapped me smiling, in my suit, my overcoat still over my arm.

It struck me that I was now the same age as Carol Park when she was murdered.

The Park family planned Carol's funeral in secret, eager to avoid media scrutiny. Jeremy and Rachael found the simple act of choosing a favourite song for their mother difficult as they realised how little they knew about her: they had been so young when she disappeared. Their mother had become 'the lady in the lake', a sobriquet they detested as they felt it removed all trace of her.

The day of the funeral arrived. Despite the Parks' efforts to keep it private, some journalists were waiting as they emerged from the service. This renewed media interest drove Park to hide away from the cameras. And so the three Park children took their mother's ashes to Birkrigg Common, a peaceful, open area of limestone countryside high above Ulverston with exquisite views over the Leven estuary. The horizon is broken by what look like the tips of broken fingers poking through the coarse grass, the remnants of a Bronze Age stone circle. Quietly and respectfully, Vanessa, Jeremy and Rachael said goodbye to the mother they had barely known and scattered her ashes on the chill wind.

A Significant Breakthrough

January, 2000

Detective Doug Marshall never gave up on justice for Carol Park. The new millennium had arrived but he could see the passing of years had brought little comfort to Ivor Price. Ivor still felt the searing pain of Carol's loss and her killer was still at large. Her tragedy had dropped out of the news headlines and seemingly out of the public consciousness. Life had moved on, while Carol was frozen in time, the victim of a hideous murder.

Out of necessity Cumbria Police had moved on, too. There were new cases to investigate. Carol's remained open, of course, and publicly the force maintained it was seeking her killer. But in real terms it wasn't top of detectives' priorities. How could it be? The murder had been thoroughly investigated at great cost. After the charge against Park was dropped, Marshall and his colleague Mike Warner had spent a further six months on the case without success. Short of a miracle, justice for Carol seemed highly unlikely.

But Doug Marshall couldn't let it go. He had been drawn in as a young Detective Constable. Years had passed since Carol's body was discovered. He was now a Detective Sergeant. In all this time he had never lost sight of the case. He was too invested now to give up.

During those intervening years, he would regularly drive out to Walney Island, slowing the car as it turned into Lord Roberts Street, knock on Ivor and Maureen Price's front door and step into their home. He would sit with them and tell them there was nothing new to report. "I had to be circumspect," Marshall said. "What you didn't want to do was engender any false hope or expectations."

Family liaison was an important part of his job, especially with a cold case such as Carol Park's. It was vital to reassure the Prices that the investigation was still important, that the police had not given up on finding the killer. Marshall knew how important this was to Ivor and his family.

He knew how badly they'd reacted to the charge being dropped against Gordon Park. "They were gutted," Marshall remembered. Shortly after, Marshall saw the resolve in Ivor Price reignite, an iron will to fight for justice. "I think it made Ivor more determined to prove things and do what he could," Marshall said. "It became a life mission."

Ivor's strength made Marshall more determined. No matter where he went, no matter what case he was working on, he carried the Carol Price file with him, always. It was like a candle flame. It might flicker, but he would never allow it to go out.

"I couldn't accept that we couldn't carry on [investigating the case]," he recalled. "A lot of work had gone into it. The evidence was still clearly pointing to Gordon Park and I got promoted to Sergeant in 1998 and I took the file with me. I carried it and I kept it in my drawer and chipped away at inquiries myself without any great remit at that point. Where I went, it went."

To all intents and purposes it was a one-man investigation. Yet it seemed an impossible task. What hope did Marshall have, working under his own steam, of succeeding?

Fate would favour DS Doug Marshall, however, and his dedication would be rewarded with a significant breakthrough.

I had left the Westmorland *Gazette* at Christmas 1999 and in the subsequent years was a staff journalist on various newspapers across the north of England. I did shifts as a sub-editor on national newspapers in Manchester and wrote features for magazines. I never lost interest in the Park case. The memories were seared too deeply into my psyche.

Now living in Cheshire, Louise and I were blessed in due course by the birth of our daughter and son. We returned regularly to the Lake District to visit my parents. These trips triggered fleeting memories of covering the Lady in the Lake case. I'd often reflect: would Carol Park's killer ever be caught? It was now almost 30 years since she had gone missing, almost a decade since her body had been discovered in Coniston Water.

In the early 2000s I found myself working on a different murder case, one that would refresh my links with coroner Ian Smith in Cumbria and unlock thoughts of Carol Park in my mind. I was now the assistant editor of the *Warrington Guardian*, responsible for a team of sub-editors and for ensuring multiple editions of the paper went to press. News broke that Warrington teenager Shafilea Ahmed, a British-Pakistani, had been murdered by her parents because she had refused an arranged marriage. Her father, a taxi driver, drove her body to Cumbria where it was found in the River Kent at Sedgwick, a village south of Kendal.

It was a disturbing case and I found myself acting as a conduit for shared information and photographs between the *Warrington Guardian* and my old newspaper the *Westmorland Gazette*. At the inquest, coroner Ian Smith described Shafilea's death as a "very vile murder".

When I was reminded of the Carol Park case on such occasions, I would do an internet search, hoping there had been a breakthrough in the hunt for her killer. I was disappointed: nothing new. Little did I know that behind the scenes detectives had had a stroke of luck.

The turning point came in October 2000 when the police received a call from a man called Michael Wainwright who said he'd shared a prison cell with Gordon Park who was on remand in 1997 after his initial arrest. In the phone call Wainwright told DS Doug Marshall that Park had confessed to killing his wife.

Marshall's pulse quickened. Potentially, this was an important breakthrough but Marshall remained wary. The man, after all, was an ex-con. Could he be trusted? Would his testimony carry weight as evidence in court?

Marshall arranged to interview Wainwright at Kendal police station. When Wainwright arrived, Marshall had to assess his credibility. Marshall looked at his record. It transpired Wainwright had been accused of assaulting his stepson and convicted before magistrates in Ormskirk in Lancashire in February 1997. He had been put on probation but when he broke its terms he had been re-sentenced to six months in

Preston Prison. Due to his conviction for a crime against a child he was considered a vulnerable prisoner. This, he told DS Marshall, was why he ended up on F Wing where Park was being held. He told the detective he had not known who Park was but remembered seeing him exercising in the prison courtyard. Other prisoners were shouting names at Park. The name that Wainwright remembered was 'Bin bags', a reference to the bags lining Carol's body in Coniston Water. Wainwright had thought no more of it until he found Park in a corner of the exercise yard mumbling to himself. Wainwright claimed he heard Park muttering, "She deserved it." When he asked Park what he meant, Wainwright claimed Park ignored the question, but on a later occasion, Park asked if he could confide in him as he had something he wished to get off his chest.

Wainwright told DS Marshall what Park had told him. Park had admitted he had killed his wife and that she had deserved it because she had been unfaithful.

Marshall listened quietly, the interview tape running in the background. Wainwright went on to describe what he claimed was Park's account of Carol's death. Park had choked her with his hands around her neck until she passed out. He had struck Carol's inert body with an implement that had a black handle and a head with an axe at one end and a pick at the other. Marshall thought it sounded like an ice axe used in rock climbing. Park had put the body in his car, Wainwright said, and driven to Coniston Water where he had taken it out in his boat.

Wainwright explained that after this confession Park had been taken away to his remand hearing and he never saw him again because Park was released on bail.

Marshall posed the obvious question to Wainwright: why had he not come forward with this evidence earlier? Wainwright claimed he feared Park might employ someone to threaten him if he did. He had finally found it in his conscience to come forward after seeing the television documentary Ladies of the Lake, which had featured Carol Park's case, in September 2000. He claimed the programme had triggered unpleasant memories of his time in prison. Struggling to sleep, he decided to clear his conscience.

DS Marshall looked at the man sitting opposite him, processing what he'd just been told. He later assessed Wainwright thus, "He was obviously a con, but he didn't present particularly badly at that time."

He thanked Wainwright, the evidence safely recorded and ready to add to the Carol Park file that accompanied him wherever he went. Was it a breakthrough? Time would tell. It generated a new possible line of inquiry: were there other prisoners who might have been privy to a prison-cell confession from Gordon Park?

"I did a lot of work with the Prison Service to find out who else had been in the cell with him," remembered Marshall. Intriguingly, he wanted to find a prisoner Wainwright had described as 'Banksy'. It wasn't much to go on but Marshall persisted and almost seven months later his investigations led to a man called Glen Banks who since his release from prison was living in Blackburn in supervised accommodation as he had learning difficulties.

In 2001, Marshall and a colleague drove to the Lancashire mill town to meet Banks. Marshall told Banks, who was with two social workers, that they were there to discuss Gordon Park.

Banks' immediate response was to say that Park had put his wife in the lake with a lead pipe. It quickly became apparent to Marshall that Banks might be suggestible due to his learning difficulties and he terminated the meeting. On 12 June 2001, Marshall returned with two colleagues, one of whom was specially trained in interviewing people with learning difficulties, to interview Banks in the presence of a social worker.

Banks said he had been on F Wing at Preston Prison for a number of months and shared his cell initially with a friend, but when he was moved on, a new cell-mate was brought in. The man, Banks recalled, was about six-foot tall and aged about 50. It was Gordon Park. He had found Park friendly. As their relationship developed, Park helped Banks with reading and writing letters.

At some point during their time together in their cell, Park said to Banks, "I should not have done it."

Banks asked what he meant. Park confessed he had killed his wife – or 'missus'.

Park paced up and down the cell, repeating that he shouldn't have done it, Banks claimed.

Marshall and his colleagues drove back to Cumbria. They knew the testimonies of Banks and Wainwright were questionable but they were the breakthrough they had been waiting for.

26

Fresh Eyes

2000-2003

With the passing years came changes in command at Cumbria CID. Among those who moved on were the senior investigating officers, Detective Superintendent Ian Douglas and Detective Chief Inspector Noel Kelly.

Doug Marshall recalled, "The bosses I had at that time in Barrow were very reticent to do anything further on this case. I don't blame them because, organisationally, in some people's eyes we had failed once and a lot of money had been put into it. They were very sceptical of whether I was going to get any further."

The tide turned when a new Detective Chief Inspector and Detective Inspector were appointed early in the new century. Marshall saw this as an opportunity to outline the case to his new superiors who would have a fresh perspective. "I said I wanted the opportunity to do a presentation," he said, "to tell them about this case and where I was up to."

To his delight, his new bosses DCI Keith Churchman and DI Geoff Huddleston agreed. And so he began putting together a summary of his recent work.

The day of the presentation arrived. The conference room at Barrow Police Station had been booked. With a sense of purpose and no doubt nerves, he loaded up his PowerPoint slides and carefully began to run through his points. Watching with Churchman and Huddleston were representatives from the Crown Prosecution Service. He carefully talked through each piece of new evidence. The audience sat quietly and when Marshall was done he waited for their verdict.

It was now almost six years since the charges against Gordon Park had been dropped and seven since his wife's body had been found. Had Marshall done enough?

His bosses were convinced. The CPS sought a second opinion from a barrister. And then all were in agreement. There was now a credible case to be made.

The case against Gordon Park was to be reopened.

Marshall was thrilled his new bosses had invested their faith in him and a new investigation. It had an invigorating effect on the team of detectives. Marshall's time was ring-fenced specifically for the Park case and a Detective Constable was assigned to work alongside him. Their work was covert for strategic reasons. "We didn't tell the media," Marshall said; they didn't want anything to jeopardise this second bite at the cherry.

Impressively, there had been a number of breakthroughs besides the confessions of Park's cell mates. Marshall had brought in a new expert to examine the rope and knot evidence first viewed in 1997 by Rodger Ide. This time, Marshall called on the services of Mike Lucas, a member of the International Guild of Knot Tyers and Forensic Science Society, who regularly gave evidence as an expert witness in criminal cases. Marshall asked him to go over the exhibits removed from Park's two homes – Bluestones and Norland Avenue – as well as from his boats. On 17 August 2000, Lucas had presented a report of his preliminary findings. It seemed he had found significant new evidence.

Lucas delivered his final report in December 2003. In his view, Gordon Park possessed knotting skills and knowledge superior to those of the average small-boat sailor. Park was proficient in 15 different knots and splices, whereas a casual amateur was likely to know only eight. The knots used to secure the body and packaging found in Coniston Water were appropriate to the job and consistent with the knowledge that Park possessed. Lucas found the series of stopper knots used on the body interesting as they were not commonly used by sailors; instead they were more likely to be used by rock climbers.

Gordon Park was a sailor and a climber.

In Mike Lucas's expert view, the knots relating to the body and those found at Park's two properties had been tied by the same person.

Marshall's new bosses decided to take a fresh look at all the original exhibits amassed in 1997. He was grateful to them, especially DCI Keith Churchman, for their enthusiasm. Marshall said of Churchman, "He took a lot of time to personally review a lot of the material, even down to reviewing the exhibits. He did a lot of due diligence in order to get his confidence in what I was putting forward at that time. I was chomping at the bit and he's having to control my expectations."

DI Geoff Huddleston later said it had been important during the reinvestigation that the team kept an open mind.

"We restarted from scratch and went through all the previously gathered evidence and developed new lines of inquiry," he recalled. "Only one suspect emerged and that was Gordon Park."

The evidence revisited included the clothing found with the body and, significantly, a rock gathered by police divers from the lake bed of Coniston Water in 1997. This was complemented by a piece of green slate found by police divers near the body site in 2004.

"Forensic science had developed," said DI Huddleston, adding that experts had new insights to offer.

The police believed the slate to be a piece of green Westmorland slate. DI Huddleston recalled that it was highly improbable to find such a piece of slate in that place without it having been deposited there from the surface of the lake. Detectives sent the sample along with the rock to an expert in geology, Dr Duncan Pirrie of Exeter University, whose work included studying the altar stone at Stonehenge. Dr Pirrie visited Bluestones and spoke to the current owner. He also went to Coniston Water and inspected rock outcrops on the eastern shoreline. He took samples from both locations to compare with the evidence.

Huddleston remembered, "He was able to give us a mineral profile. Analysing that and with samples from Bluestones he was able to say that that rock was more likely to come from Bluestones and certainly was unlike any rock in composition and sediment from the shores of the lake."

DCI Keith Churchman later said he believed the rock and the slate had been taken to the lake with Carol's body.

The detectives were building a compelling case. Churchman said, "We were never saying this is the one piece of evidence that convicts Gordon Park. We were saying this piece of evidence supports the case *against* Gordon Park."

The time was approaching when police would once more knock on Park's front door. But having failed once, detectives were leaving nothing to chance. For months, they made detailed and meticulous plans for the anticipated interviews with Park. Hours and hours were spent drilling teams of officers to question Park on different aspects of the case. For example, one pair of detectives focused on the circumstances around the murder, while another concentrated on the knots, and so on. With such hyperfocus, each pair became experts in their area. This sophisticated strategic planning would reduce the likelihood of Park controlling the narrative during the interviews.

Marshall and his DI Geoff Huddleston prepared for the 'challenge' interviews. This is where everything that's said in all the previous interviews is brought together in order to challenge any points where they identified discrepancies. "This was a forerunner of the type of interviewing process now used today," said Marshall. "I had never put such detailed planning into a set of interviews before."

Undertaking such preparation was a mammoth task. It required detectives revisiting witnesses from the original investigation, including the forensic experts such as Home Office pathologist Dr Edmund Tapp.

The year 2003 came to a close. Cumbria CID was ready. The detectives had the prison confessions and new forensic evidence relating to Carol's clothes, the ropes and the rocks. It was time to call on Gordon Park.

27

A Detective Calls

Just before 8 o'clock in the morning on Tuesday, 14 January 2004, with the winter light slow to break the day, seven police vehicles arrived without fanfare at Norland Avenue in Hawcoat, Barrow. Detectives had come for Gordon Park, now aged 59, who was oblivious inside his home. A cordon was set up in the street to prevent any interference with what was about to happen.

Detectives Churchman and Huddleston knocked on Park's front door. Their visit was a surprise for the retired school teacher. The officers stepped into the house. Inside they informed Park he was being rearrested for the murder of his first wife Carol.

DCI Keith Churchman remembered, "He didn't say anything straight to me, no real surprise, no reaction whatsoever, certainly no fear in his eyes." He was surprised that Park's main concern was to have a shower and get dressed before being taken to the police station. The detectives allowed Park this dignity but it led to a bizarre moment which DI Huddleston recalled, "He came out of the bathroom where myself and other officers were stood and he was naked. He was carrying a towel in his hand. He made no attempt to conceal himself, in fact quite the reverse and proceeded to walk about and get dressed in the bedroom."

At 8.30am police had to prevent a man and woman from breaking the police cordon. It was reported in newspapers that the couple were friends or family of Park and that the man had become angry and tried to barge through the police cordon but was calmed down by the woman.

Park was taken to a police vehicle outside his home and in the early January morning light was driven to Barrow Police Station.

DCI Churchman was confident his team of detectives were fully prepared for the interviews that lay ahead. "We decided this time we would be in control of the interviews," he remembered. "The interviews are the opportunity for the police to ask questions of the suspect, not the other way round."

As Barrow was waking up to a new day, Cumbria Police issued a statement to say Gordon Park was "helping police with their inquiries".

"I am delighted by the news," Ivor Price told reporters. "It's what I had always hoped for. The finale might now be in sight."

Meanwhile, police searched Park's Norland Avenue home. As they had done in 1997, they removed ropes and cords from the house and the garage. They also found an ice axe and took it away.

Park was subjected to round after round of questioning by four teams of detectives using the system Marshall and his colleagues had been developing. The 'challenge' interviews were conducted by Marshall with DI Geoff Huddleston. They asked Park about the infidelities on both sides in his marriage to Carol. He was asked about the wife-swapping incident.

DS Marshall asked whether Park had known who the men were.

"She had a free rein," Park replied. "I don't actually seek to control people. It's futile, isn't it, if you are living with someone. They will do what they want to do."

He added, "I was never asked [by Carol] 'Can I do this, can I do that?' If she wanted to go out with friends, then great."

Park said he was never happy with Carol going out with male friends "unless I knew their intentions were noble".

Huddleston said, "So it wasn't an open marriage?"

"Well, I thought it was."

Huddleston asked, "So was it an open marriage as far as both of you were concerned or just her?"

Park replied, "I thought it was an open marriage. I thought it was an honest marriage between the two of us. Open to each other in that sense."

Park claimed Carol had slept with a number of men. He claimed he later learned they included a Barrow police officer as well as a Furness solicitor.

He talked about her leaving him for David Brearley and setting up home in Middlesbrough. He described the occasion at Bluestones when she had become hysterical and Brearley came from the North East to collect her.

DS Marshall asked him, "Was that a run-of-the-mill incident for you or was that something out of the ordinary or was it a regular thing in your marriage?"

"No," replied Park. "No, definitely not. This was probably

the only time I have ever had to do that. We didn't do this. We are civilised people."

The detectives asked Park about the day Carol went missing. He dismissed their suggestions she had been ill on the day he took the children to Blackpool. Instead, he told them she had refused to go and he wasn't going to force her. DI Huddleston asked whether the children had found it strange she had not joined them.

"No," Park replied, "I can't remember them asking."

He was asked if their children had been upset by her disappearance.

"Well, they weren't in floods of tears every night," he said. "The children were accustomed to daddy looking after them on his own, unfortunately. This was not a new thing for me or them."

On the question of her disappearance, the detectives asked Park why he left it six weeks to report her missing.

"I can see in retrospect this does not look good," he said.

Park sat across the desk from the detectives just as he had done in 1997 but now he was faced with fresh evidence being put to him.

A statement made by Glen Banks, the prisoner with learning difficulties, was read to Park by one of the officers.

"He states that... I'll read it to you: 'He told me that he put his wife in a black bin bag with weights in it to weigh the body down. He told me he then put the body in the bag with weights over the side of the boat and into the water.'"

"Nonsense," replied Park.

The detective continued.

Banks had claimed Park told him he'd returned from disposing of the body and his children had asked where their mother was. Park had told them she wasn't coming back, according to Banks.

"Fantasy," replied Park.

The detective read the next part of Banks's statement, "'The next day Park took the kids to Blackpool'. And that's the part that really sticks with him, apparently."

The officer looked across at Park and asked, "Did you tell him that?"

"No."

"Did you describe any trips to Blackpool with your children?"

"No."

"None?"

"I did not discuss any details of the case with anyone at Preston Prison," Park snapped.

The detectives shuffled the papers, then said, "So this person, from your point of view, has told a pack of lies?"

"I'm astonished," said Park. "I can see no sense in this at all."

The detective said, "Unless he's telling the truth. Which I suspect he is."

Park looked at his accuser. "He isn't," he replied.

Park was questioned about the ice axe. He said the one seized from his home on Norland Avenue was the only one he had ever owned. It had a wooden shaft, rather than a metal one, he told detectives, making it suitable only for snow and ice rather than rock climbing.

He was asked about the knots, ropes and cords recovered. He had learned the range of sophisticated knots and stoppers during his time in the Scouts. He denied that he had tied the ones associated with the body.

In one of the interviews, DCI Keith Churchman spoke

directly to the retired schoolteacher, "I put it to you, Mr Park, that the evidence against you is overwhelming and I urge you to think about your position carefully."

Park stared blankly.

"Please remember the caution," Churchman continued. "This is your chance to present the police with your version of events that happened on or about the 16th July 1976. Is there any further explanation you'd like to give us?"

Park was unemotional.

"No, thank you."

"Is there anything further you'd like to add or clarify?" asked Churchman.

"No, thank you."

Churchman turned to Huddleston and asked, "Geoff, any further questions?"

Huddleston looked at Park and said, "You murdered Carol Park."

Park looked from Churchman to Huddleston and asked, "Is that a question?"

"You murdered Carol Park, didn't you?" Huddleston asked. "Yes or no?"

There was a long pause from Park.

"No," he replied.

Marshall remembered Park becoming irritated at times during the interviews, "He was not a man sitting there screaming or having temper tantrums but instead was guarded."

When Marshall interviewed him about the knots, Park would demonstrate with a length of rope how to tie knots. He seemed keen to display his expertise in that regard. Twenty years on, Marshall still recalled Park showing him how to tidily gather a long piece of rope by wrapping it around his elbow. "In the intervening years, if I've ever had to tie something I've always had it going round my elbow," Marshall said.

Police were granted a 12-hour extension by Barrow magistrates late on Wednesday afternoon to continue questioning Park, a development that made front-page news in the *North West Evening Mail*, which featured a haunting full-page, three column photograph of 64-year-old Ivor Price accompanied by the headline: 'Living hell of murder victim's brother'.

Those extra 12 hours were intensive and relentless. Detectives were not going to allow anything to get in the way of their goal. The extension would run out at 7am on Thursday, taking the length of time Park had been in custody to 36 hours. There would be the possibility to extend further after which detectives would have to either charge Park or release him.

As it turned out, detectives did not apply for an extra extension. They had made a resolution: they would charge 59-year-old Gordon Park. It was following the final interview on 15 January.

Doug Marshall, now Detective Sergeant, had the task of formally putting the charge of murder to Park. It was a distinction Marshall would later recall, "I've charged the same man with the same murder twice."

Gordon Park, who was 10 days away from his 60th birthday, said nothing in response.

Jeremy and Rachael Park were devastated when they heard of their father's re-arrest.

Jeremy had just climbed out of the bath when he received an early morning phone call from Jenny. She told him what had happened: Park had been taken away. The police had gone through the house removing paperwork, computers, photographs, CDs and lengths of string,

Jeremy felt a terrible darkness descend. The nightmare they'd lived through seven years earlier had returned. Rachael Park was pregnant and living in Beijing with her husband and it would be months before she was able to return to England. When she did arrive home she was shaken by the state of her father: he looked much older and was downcast and preoccupied and spent much of his time shuffling through the case papers.

28

"I hope that's not his wife"

On Friday, 16 January 2004 the judicial process was reset. Almost seven years on from his last court appearance, Park was brought before a special hearing at Furness and District Magistrates' Court, presided over not by magistrates but by a district judge because of the exceptional circumstances.

The court stands on Abbey Road, the long arterial road through the heart of Barrow. It is ugly and made of brick, pressed up against a handsome older sandstone building that features words in bright red capital letters: 'THE SALVATION ARMY'.

Park's hopes of salvation were fast running out.

He wore a maroon blazer in an echo of his first appearance in 1997 when he was first charged with Carol's murder. Was it the same blazer?

The hearing started at 10am and Park touched the microphone in the dock before he took his seat. He was impassive for most of the 40-minute hearing, a solemn expression on his face. From time to time he glanced across at the packed public gallery and press bench. On occasions he took deep breaths and turned his eyes to the ceiling of the court.

The detectives, who a few hours earlier had been questioning him, watched from the public gallery. Sitting alongside them were Ivor and Maureen Park. Notably absent was Park's wife, Jenny.

The only time Park spoke was when he confirmed his name and address. His solicitor was once more Mike Graham, who made an application for bail, telling the judge that the £20,000 surety was "easily achievable" for his client. As Graham spoke, Park leaned forward in his dock seat to listen closely.

The judge granted Park bail. A date was set for the pre-trial hearings to begin on 11 February at Preston Crown Court. As Park left the dock he clenched his fists by his side and nodded to people he knew in the public gallery. He made a quick exit from the court and was pictured by photographers climbing into a green car a little further along Abbey Road from the court building.

Reporters approached Park's solicitor Mike Graham and DS Doug Marshall as they emerged onto Abbey Road but both said they would not be making statements. Only Ivor Price stopped to speak to journalists. He described his relief at the charges against Park and praised detectives for not giving up on trying to catch his sister's killer.

Newspapers speculated that Gordon Park might end up in the record books as the person to be charged the longest time after the victim had died. Paul Williams of true crime website Murderfile.com told reporters that because of the advent of

DNA evidence more and more defendants were being brought to justice decades after the crimes.

Park had been charged 27 years and six months after Carol went missing. Williams said, "The Lady in the Lake case is rare but not unique."

The long journey to the trial of Gordon Park had begun.

Newspaper headlines about Park's arrest led to another stroke of luck for detectives. A middle-aged couple called Jean and John Young, who lived in Scotland, got in touch with what turned out to be a remarkable story, stacking further circumstantial evidence against Park.

It was now almost 30 years after the fact, but the couple told detectives that in July 1976 they had been on holiday in the Lake District, staying in the pretty market town of Keswick. John had suffered a torn cartilage and was using crutches to get about. During the course of their holiday, John had proposed to Jean.

This is why the events they were about to witness had stuck in their memory.

Two or three days into their holiday, they decided to drive from Keswick to the village of Hawkshead and thereafter on to Coniston Water. It was late in the morning and they followed the road along the eastern shore before reaching a pleasant spot in a car park, where they pulled up to enjoy the glorious view across the lake. They had brought copies of that day's newspapers with them and wanted to enjoy the tranquillity while they caught up on the news.

It was a very quiet spot; Jean told detectives there were very few other people about. The only movement they noticed was a white boat gently cutting through the surface of the lake.

Curious, Jean picked up a pair of binoculars, put them to

her eyes and watched the boat. It stopped and Jean could see a figure doing something industrious onboard. The figure was a youngish man with a thin face, brown or auburn hair, who was wearing glasses, and was dressed in a wetsuit, so she had assumed he was a diver.

It had stuck in her mind because the man kept glancing across at their car on the edge of the lake. Jean wondered why he was so interested in them.

"That was what made me keep looking at him," she later recalled. With hindsight, she wondered whether the man was trying to establish if there was someone in their car. She could see he was handling a large object; it looked like a rolled-up carpet. The man picked it up.

If he was a diver, she wondered whether he was trying to hoist air tanks onto his back. But when he toppled the object over the side of the boat into the lake she realised she must have been mistaken.

The object vanished below the surface of the water.

John had also been watching, piqued by Jean's interest.

"He must be dumping an old carpet or some heavy rubbish," Jean thought. She turned to John and asked him what he thought.

And then she joked, "I hope that's not his wife."

Jean and John drove off shortly afterwards but they continued to think about what they'd witnessed. For weeks afterwards they checked newspapers and television news bulletins, not quite sure what they were looking for, but keen not to miss an explanation of what they'd seen.

Something didn't feel right but what could they do? So, they didn't report what they'd seen to the police.

In 1998, 22 years after the incident, Jean and John – now Mr and Mrs Young – were once again on holiday in Keswick. Jean happened to see a newspaper cutting on the wall in their hotel. It was a report about the 'Lady in the Lake' case, most likely about the charges against Gordon Park being dropped. She assumed this meant that Park was not guilty. Again, she and John did not report what they'd seen to police.

But at last, in January 2004, Jean Young heard about the re-arrest of Gordon Park and contacted the police to give a formal witness statement. In the meantime, she had seen a photograph online of Gordon Park. Despite the fact that Park would have been almost 30 years older in the picture, Jean felt sure he and the man she'd seen in 1976 were one and the same.

DI Geoff Huddleston later recalled, "When the Youngs got in touch I must admit there was probably nobody more cynical in the office than yours truly."

DCI Keith Churchman said, "Of course it did cross our minds had Mr and Mrs Young seen Gordon Park and would he be stupid enough to dispose of Carol during the day. But knowing Gordon Park's character and the way he didn't like to take risks the best time for him not to be disturbed or not to be identified as doing something covert would be by going on that lake during the day the way he'd done many times before on Coniston and Windermere. So it doesn't surprise me and it isn't out of character with him."

The Youngs' testimony was "the icing on the cake" so close to the trial, as far as Huddleston was concerned.

29

God and my Right

It was cold in Manchester on the morning of Monday, 22 November 2004.

Sixty-year-old Gordon Park arrived at the Crown Court in Crown Square, holding hands with his wife Jenny. He wore a dark brown leather jacket, white shirt and a blue tie, and black woollen gloves to keep out the winter chill. Over his shoulder he carried a blue and green rucksack. Inevitably, he was shadowed by photographers and camera crews as he and Jenny approached the sombre white concrete building. Park did not smile and lowered his gaze, weaving through concrete pillars at the entrance. Above his head were the words 'Manchester Crown Court (Crown Square)' and the British Royal Coat of Arms depicting a lion, a unicorn, a crown and the phrase 'Dieu et mon droit'. *God and my right.*

He had entered a not-guilty plea at Preston Crown Court in February. Today was the first day of his trial. The hearing had been ear-marked to last 10 weeks. For the duration of the trial, Park would stay in Manchester with Pastor George Harrison of the Pendlebury Evangelical Church, whose son taught at the same school as Jenny Park in Cumbria.

Ten months had passed since Park's arrest. Given the complexity of the case and the amount of evidence, the delay was to be expected. Park had been on bail during this limbo period.

There was huge media interest and the public gallery was packed.

Presiding over the trial in Court 4 was the Honourable Mr Justice McCombe. In his early 50s, Richard McCombe had been educated privately in the Lake District at Sedbergh School before going on to Cambridge. He was the Presiding Judge on the Northern Circuit and was an imposing figure in his judge's gown and wig, his face dominated by luxuriant eyebrows.

The barristers making the case for the Crown Prosecution Service were Alistair Webster QC and Kate Blackwell. Webster was 52 and had followed his father, a judge, into the profession. He spoke with a rich, mellifluous voice and was an experienced prosecutor described by Chambers, the legal guide to barristers, as a "tactical genius". Blackwell, aged 35, had been part of the legal team that prosecuted serial killer Dr Harold Shipman in 2000 and subsequently represented Greater Manchester Police at the public inquiry into the case.

The defence team representing Park was led by Andrew Edis QC, who was 47, and from Liverpool. In the coming years he would become well known as the lead prosecutor in the phone hacking trial following allegations relating to tabloid newspaper practices, the scandal that saw Rupert Murdoch close the *News of the World*. Supporting Edis was junior defence counsel Brian Williams.

If the press were expecting courtroom fireworks, they were

disappointed during the opening three days of the trial. These sessions were dedicated to dry rounds of legal discussions.

The judge listened as defence barrister Andrew Edis argued that the evidence in which Jean Young identified a recent photo of Gordon Park should be excluded from the trial. McCombe agreed and prevented it from being put before the jury, which had yet to be sworn in. Edis also requested McCombe exclude the evidence from Park's one-time prison contemporaries Michael Wainwright and Glen Banks on the grounds that the relevant prison records were missing. McCombe declined to grant this request: Wainwright's and Banks's testimonies would be heard by jurors. Edis made a series of further requests regarding prosecution evidence but by the end of Wednesday, the judge signalled it was time to get the trial of Gordon Park under way.

The seven women and five men of the jury were sworn in on the morning of Thursday, 25 November. They were watched by Gordon Park, who was sitting in the dock.

The court fell silent as Alistair Webster QC, resplendent in his wig and gown, rose from his seat and began to outline the Crown's case.

"Whoever killed and disposed of Carol Park," he told the jury, "would have the following characteristics: a person who knew her sufficiently well to come across her in her short nightdress; a person who had reason to strongly dislike her or lose his temper with her; a person who was thoroughly familiar with knots, both as a sailor and a climber; a meticulous person; a person with access to a boat and familiarity with Coniston Water."

The jury listened intently.

Webster said, "One man fits this description: Gordon Park."

The brutality of Carol Park's death was starkly laid out, the details of which would shortly be divulged in press and broadcast reports sent across the globe.

Webster said, "The remains of her skull showed that she had been attacked, and that her face had been shattered by a number of blows, and that a sharp-edged instrument had been involved.

"Ironically, if Gordon Park had dropped [her body] over the side of his boat a few feet further out, it would have gone much deeper. She was, in effect, lying at the top of an underwater slope. It is unlikely that she would have ever been found."

Gordon Park sat feet away, listening to Alistair Webster's coruscating accusations against him.

The jury was told about the Parks' unhappy marriage and their mutual infidelity. They were told of the protracted battle over custody of the children and Carol's return to Bluestones for their sake.

Webster delicately explained the terrible tragedies that had befallen the Price family, the traumatic murder of Christine, and of the Parks' adoption of Vanessa.

He spoke of the six-week gap Park left before reporting Carol's disappearance.

"Questions were bound to be asked," he said. "He [Park] had no choice but to report her missing."

The new evidence that had come to light since 1998 was outlined.

There was the testimony of Jean and John Young and there were the apparent confessions by Park to fellow inmates at Preston Prison.

Webster observed that Park's friends and family would find it difficult to believe he "has carried this dark secret for so many years".

Bringing his opening remarks to a close, Alistair Webster told the jury: "We do not suggest that any one single piece of evidence points indisputably to the defendant being the killer. The care with which he disposed of the body and concealed his crime for so many years meant that the police have carefully had to sift through the evidence – a painstaking process."

The hearing was adjourned to the following morning. Gordon Park walked briskly out of the court with Jenny by his side, photographers snapping fresh images for the evening's late editions.

30

Prosecution

And so the trial settled into a rhythm.

Each day Park and Jenny walked into court to be met by the waiting legal teams and a packed public gallery and press bench. Each day the jury filed in and the judge re-adjourned the hearing.

One by one, Crown prosecutor Webster began to call his long list of witnesses, expert or otherwise, to the stand. He would lead them through his carefully choreographed questions before sitting down to allow cross-examination by the defence's Andrew Edis.

The first witness was Ivor Price. He and his wife Maureen, who spoke later, told the court of the last occasions they'd seen Carol, the children's performance at Barrow Town Hall when she had seemed subdued.

Home Office pathologist Dr Edmund Tapp delivered the findings from his post-mortem examination of Carol's remains. He spoke in precise terms, his testimony a stomach-churning experience for the members of the jury. He talked about the body's white, soapy appearance, due to its exposure to water for so long, a process known as adipocere.

He explained that a piece of medical dressing had been discovered, with hairs from the eyebrows and eyelashes, suggesting Carol's eyes had been taped over.

Tapp told jurors the body must have been trussed up in the foetal position within two to three hours of death — any later and rigor mortis would have made it impossible.

Webster called on Rodger Ide, the expert who had first examined the rope evidence in 1997, in place of Michael Lucas, who had provided the more recent report in 2003. Philip Rydeard testified in relation to the lead piping and a statement was read out from facial reconstruction specialist Caroline Wilkinson of the University of Manchester.

The jury was told about further evidence gathered by the police: the toilet pan, the well-used claw hammer and the wooden ice axe.

The geology expert Dr Duncan Pirrie who had examined the rock and slate recovered from Coniston Water explained the comparisons made with samples recovered from the wall at Bluestones and the eastern shoreline of the lake.

The slate was typical of the type used across South Cumbria for roofing and was not unusual. The rock was another matter, however.

He told the jury, "It is possible, in some circumstances, to identify stones which are indigenous to the lake bed and adjoining areas. When the lake bed was examined, stones were recovered which did not originate from Coniston.

"They did, however, match stones from one of the walls at Bluestones, the house that Gordon Park built."

The same rock sample had also been examined by the defence expert, Dr Kenneth Pye, who believed the similarity was not as suspicious as it might appear. In Pye's view, the rock was of glacial origin, and examples were commonly found widely spread across the bottom of Coniston Water and along its shore and surrounding landscape. Edis would use this evidence to show the jury it was wrong to draw the conclusion the rock had been brought from Bluestones.

Webster called upon the woman who believed she had seen Carol Park at Charnock Richard service station on 17 July 1976. The married woman, who had known Ivor Price and Carol in the 1970s through church, had originally reported the sighting to police in 1976 but frustratingly her statement had been lost along with the case file from that time. Since then, having checked diaries and calendars, she now believed she had been mistaken about the precise date.

Jean and John Young spoke about the strange incident they witnessed on Coniston Water in 1976. The jury heard how the police had taken the Youngs back to the lake in 2004 to pinpoint the scene of the sighting: it was around a mile from where the body was found.

The Youngs' description of the man they saw would in due course be put to Park when he took the stand. It would lead to a moment of courtroom drama later in the trial.

Webster called DS Doug Marshall to describe the police investigation over the years since 1997. Marshall had been the only detective who had worked continuously on the case from the moment of the body's discovery. His testimony at Manchester Crown Court was well-rehearsed: he had given evidence at Park's four pre-trial hearings.

Marshall and his colleague Mike Wallace, who had also worked closely on the investigation, decamped to Manchester for the duration of the trial. During the week they stayed in the Victoria and Albert Hotel and returned home at weekends. The hotel was in Water Street, close to Granada Television Studios, where *Coronation Street* was filmed. The two detectives became used to seeing famous actors drinking in the hotel bar. Marshall remembers Liz Dawn, who played Mancunian big-mouth Vera Duckworth, learning her lines in the bar. She joked that they couldn't read her confidential script as it was for a forthcoming episode. She had no idea who the detectives were and they were duty-bound not to discuss the trial.

The most startling moment during the Crown's case came when Vanessa Park gave evidence for the prosecution against her adoptive father.

Now aged 36, she testified that she had no recollection of visiting Blackpool in the summer of 1976, the trip that Gordon Park had maintained took place on the day Carol went missing. This revelation cast doubt on the veracity of Park's account.

Vanessa told the jury her father had been strict; she remembered him striking her and her siblings with a stick. She could only recall this period in snapshots, like a flickering home movie. She remembered with affection a holiday with her mother and David Brearley in Middlesbrough. She remembered returning to Bluestones at the end of the holiday, collected by Park. She could also remember that her mother travelled home with them.

Park displayed no emotion as he listened to his daughter speak.

Webster also called Jeremy and Rachael to give evidence but unlike Vanessa, they spoke up in favour of their father.

Both had been very young at the time of their mother's disappearance but each had certain vivid 'snapshot' memories of Carol. They recalled the holidays with her and Brearley in Middlesbrough. In contrast to Vanessa's memories, Jeremy did recall the trip to Blackpool on Saturday, 17 July 1976. He told the court the last time he saw his mother was that morning. It had been planned as a family trip but Carol had said she didn't want to go. He had tried to persuade her but she had not been keen, he recalled. This had left him feeling rejected by his mother. He had clear memories of the visit: he could remember going on the Wild Mouse ride.

He also disagreed with Vanessa over their father's approach to discipline: Park had only ever used his hand, never a stick, Jeremy maintained. Meanwhile, during cross-examination by Alistair Webster, Rachael recanted a statement she gave to police in 1997 to the effect that Park had used a belt to discipline them. Now, on the stand, she told the court she could not recall ever being hit with anything other than her father's hand. "I was traumatised during the whole of this," she told the court. "My father was in prison, the media was camping on my doorstep, my mother had just been murdered... probably the police put words into my mouth."

Rachael would tell the jury, "He is a loving, supportive, kind, fantastic father."

Alistair Webster called Michael Wainwright and Glen Banks to testify that Park had confessed to killing Carol while at Preston Prison.

Wainwright explained what Park had told him, where and when. Defence barrister Andrew Edis cross-examined him in great detail at length about the limited contact Wainwright would have had with Park and the likelihood of such a confession being made. Edis picked up on inconsistencies in Wainwright's statements: for example, Wainwright claimed Park had said he had climbed a set of stairs during the attack on Carol, yet Bluestones is a bungalow. Edis was also keen to ask about Wainwright's long-term abuse of drugs such as amphetamine, cocaine and LSD and the inevitable impact on his memory.

Due to his vulnerability, Glen Banks gave evidence via a video link. He told the jury exactly what he'd told Detective Doug Marshall. During cross-examination, Andrew Edis highlighted certain discrepancies in Banks's testimony, including his claim that he had shared a cell with Park for a number of months, when in fact Park had been on remand for 14 days.

November melted into December and Christmas loomed. The trial adjourned for the festive period and resumed in the first week of the new year, when Alistair Webster QC concluded the prosecution case for the Crown. These days were dedicated to hearing about Carol Park's relationship with David Brearley, who – now in his 50s – attended court as a prosecution witness and gave evidence on the stand. He told the court of their relationship, recounting how Carol had gone back to Park and how it had been a tumultuous time in his life.

He was asked under cross-examination by Andrew Edis how their relationship had ended.

Brearley replied, "It was like the end of a nightmare. Like going to the dentist for an operation. You know it is going to be bad but once it is over you realise it was a blessed relief."

The witnesses for the prosecution had been heard. It was time for the defence of Gordon Park to begin.

31

Love's Young
Dream

Park's barrister Andrew Edis QC told the jury that 12 witnesses for the defence would be called. There would be character testimonies from Jeremy and Rachael and his wife, Jenny. But the witness most keenly anticipated would be Gordon Park himself.

Before that, however, there was a significant matter to undertake. The jurors had requested they be allowed to visit the locations at the heart of the trial. So, on Tuesday, 11 January, along with Judge McCombe, the jury of seven women and five men made the 100-mile trip north from Manchester to Cumbria to see Coniston Water and the hamlet of Leece. Significantly, Gordon Park would be travelling too. His return sent the newspapers into paroxysms of excitement.

A minibus transported the jurors to meet with the judge and barristers Webster and Edis at Greenodd. This village sits on the A590 east of Ulverston overlooking the pretty River Leven estuary.

Press photographers captured the fleeting moments at Greenodd when a stern-faced Park could be seen taking a call on his mobile phone wearing a heavy winter coat and cream trousers.

Reporters later noted the judge and barristers had exchanged formal court robes for warm winter clothing as a convoy of the minibus and six dark saloon cars ventured into the winter embrace of the Lake District.

To allow the court party to make their visit without interference from journalists and Leece's 300 residents, police blocked off the roads in and out of the tiny hamlet. Jurors and lawyers climbed out of their vehicles in Leece and turned their attention to the whitewashed bungalow Bluestones, which overlooks the tarn at the heart of the community. They spent 20 minutes quietly walking around the property without actually going inside. Park was among them, back at the bungalow he had built almost 40 years earlier. Newspapers later published a picture of him in a black woollen hat and gloves walking up the narrow lane to Bluestones. His return was brief and he stepped back and stood on the steep drive as the jurors made their inspection.

That evening the *North West Evening Mail* used the images of Park on its front page with the headline: 'PARK RETURNS TO LEECE HOME'.

The party returned to the minibus at lunchtime to be taken to Coniston Water, an hour's drive away. The weather deteriorated; heavy rain and fog settled in. The jurors stared out of the minibus at the starkly beautiful Lakeland scenery. The lonely country lanes were empty. This was a landscape that had been battered by storms only days earlier. The minibus paused at

Machell's Coppice, a viewing point overlooking the lake where the Youngs claimed to have seen Park push a large object into the water.

The jurors climbed out to take a closer look and spent 10 minutes peering across the choppy surface of the lake. Guiding the party was PC Steve Carruthers of the North West Police Underwater Search Unit, who had been part of the diving team that scoured the lake bed in 1997. He answered jurors' questions under the direction of the judge, Richard McCombe, who sheltered underneath a golfing umbrella, his glasses speckled with raindrops.

Some of the jurors used binoculars to look across the lake but the weather worsened and they found themselves squinting through driving rain. They were ushered back to the minibus and were whisked a mile further along the eastern edge of the lake. They stopped at Bailiff Wood. This was where Carol Park's body had been found by the Kendal divers seven and a half years earlier.

Low clouds haloed the fell-tops overlooking the lake. A deluge of rain and biting wind forced the party to huddle under umbrellas as they gazed again across the surface of the lake. The only thing breaking the surface was an orange buoy bobbing 200 metres from the shore. It had been placed by police divers to indicate where the body had been found. It was an eerie sight.

There was no more to see. The weather had closed in; the light had thinned. The party returned to their vehicles. The jurors were driven back to Manchester and dismissed for the day. The hearing would resume at the city's Crown Court the following morning. Gordon Park was due to take the stand.

Wednesday, 12 January.

It was the moment the public and the press had been waiting for. Gordon Park stepped into the witness box. He was dressed in a dark grey pinstripe suit, white shirt and a purple tie. In contrast to the sombre-faced man from press photographs, Park was remarkably relaxed for someone in his position. As he began to speak, he made little jokes to the jury about being unable to recall past events.

His barrister, Andrew Edis began by asking about his marriage to Carol. Park spoke in a quiet voice and on a couple of occasions, Edis asked him to speak up. Reporters later noted that Park spoke fondly about Carol. Each of Edis's questions elicited an answer from Park that, no doubt, had been practised in preparation for the trial.

It was the first occasion Park had spoken publicly – not to a reporter but actually within the presence of other people – about his marriage, the summer of 1976 and the terrible allegations against him.

Edis asked how he'd met Carol.

"I was working at the time," Park said, "and she was at the town hall. She must have been 17 and I must have been 18."

They had known each other only a short period when they became romantically involved and, shortly afterwards, engaged.

"I was in love with her," he told the jury. "I loved her, and she me. Wonderful. Love's young dream."

Love's young dream: it was a headline writer's dream and was milked in the evening editions.

Edis asked him about subjects that would show elements of his good character. Park discussed his success and popularity as a school teacher; he took pride in his achievements in raising his family as a single parent.

Park spoke of the 11 months prior to Carol's disappearance. This was a time when she had returned to him at Bluestones. She seemed happy, he told the jury. He believed they had been rebuilding their relationship. He had begun to trust her once more.

Edis moved on to the events of Saturday, 17 July 1976. Park gave his account of the day: that morning Carol had said she was unwell and would not join them on a family trip to Blackpool, so he had taken Vanessa, Jeremy and Rachael on his own. Carol was not at home when they returned; there was no sign of a disturbance at their home. Her rings were on her dressing table. He did not discuss Carol's disappearance with anyone: he assumed she had gone off with another man.

Edis asked Park about Bluestones and in particular the stones of the walls around the bungalow. Park said rubble from the cottages demolished on the plot of land had been repurposed by Carol's uncle Arnold. "The rubble came from them to build the walls," Park said. It was an answer designed to address the evidence recovered by police divers from Coniston Water.

Park admitted he had been a keen sailor and climber. He admitted he had sailed regularly on Coniston Water and owned a number of boats.

He denied killing his wife.

He denied tying the knots associated with the body.

He denied visiting the location where the body was found, although he admitted it was opposite where his family had kept a caravan during his childhood.

Edis asked Park to address the prison cell confessions alleged by Wainwright and Banks. Park said they had been fabricated. He said he'd had no interaction with Wainwright and had not discussed his case with Banks.

It was time for Park to face cross-examination from prosecutor Alistair Webster. The ensuing confrontation was electric, leaving reporters frantically scribbling in their notebooks.

Webster challenged Park on his treatment of Carol during their marriage and also on the events of 17 July 1976.

Park admitted he had lied under oath at the custody hearing when Carol was living with David Brearley. He'd denied having an extra-marital affair when questioned at the children's custody hearing, when in fact he was seeing Judith Walmsley.

"I thought it would jeopardise my chances of getting custody of the children," he told the court.

Webster leapt on this admission as it showed something important about Park's character.

"When you told a lie about your relationship with Judith Walmsley you lied under oath," said Webster.

"Yes, I did," answered Park.

"You also gave evidence under oath?"

"Ah, yes," admitted Park.

"Ah, yes," mocked Webster. "What did you tell the court about your relationship?"

"That there was no adultery," replied Park.

"So you lied on oath?" said Webster. "You did, didn't you?"

Uncomfortably, Park responded, "Yes, I did."

Park was a man prepared to tell lies under oath in a courtroom.

Webster suggested cracks first emerged in the marriage when Carol discovered he took contraceptives around with him.

"Why would you carry contraceptives in your pocket?" asked Webster.

"We used to make love wherever we felt like it," said Park.

Webster turned his attention to the notorious wife-swapping incident in 1974. Park explained he and Carol had been at a house with another couple from Barrow. He said, "We all knew what was going on. I found myself in a bedroom with [the other wife]. We had a bit of a go and that was that."

Webster turned to the events of July 1976 and Carol's disappearance. Why had Park taken so long to raise the alarm?

"The fact she didn't leave a note implied to me she didn't want me to know where she was," said Park. "By the morning I had it in my head she had left again, probably with another person."

After a moment, Park added, "I'm guilty of self-pity. Yes, if I had acted sooner and thought she was a missing person she may have been located in time... I'm guilty of neglect, of not having enough care for my wife."

"You are guilty of rather more than that," Webster retorted sharply

"No, Mr Webster," Park replied, "I'm not guilty of anything more than that."

Park told the court he couldn't sleep the night Carol disappeared, "I was waiting for the phone call, sound of a car door, her footsteps on the drive and wondering whether she was in another bed somewhere."

Webster asked why, in the days afterwards, Park hadn't asked Ivor Price whether Carol had been in touch with him.

"I was expecting to hear from Carol before the holidays were over, that is what I expected," Park responded.

Webster then questioned Park over his decision to speak to his solicitors, Forresters in Barrow, rather than first going to the police to report Carol missing.

Park replied, "Forresters knew the full history, all the matrimonial problems. I was unsure what to do so I rang them seeking advice. You seek advice when you are not sure what to do."

Webster asked about a box Park had given to a friend when police were gathering evidence from his home. Park said there was "nothing sinister" in the box: it contained tapes of Buddhist lectures from Ulverston's Manjushri Meditation Centre and he'd been concerned he might not see them again if the police took them.

Of the police's claims Park turned to Buddhism to deal with his guilt over killing Carol, Park said, "It was such a fatuous allegation, there was no evidence to hide. It's the police clutching at straws."

Webster asked Park about the Youngs' sighting of a man on a white boat, dropping a large object into the lake. Park admitted his boat at the time had been white and he conceded he would have had a full head of auburn hair in 1976. But he said he did not wear glasses outside at that time, only when he was reading.

Park was shown a photograph of himself that had the date inscribed on the reverse: 25 August 1973. It showed Park wearing glasses outside. A shocked Park admitted he was surprised to see himself wearing spectacles in those circumstances.

Webster asked Park if he'd owned a wetsuit in that period. Park admitted he had owned one in 1976 but it had been damaged on a sailing course at least a month before Carol disappeared.

Webster asked Park if he had spoken to his adopted daughter Vanessa since she had decided to give evidence for the prosecution.

"No," replied Park.

"Did she send you any Christmas presents?"

"Yes, but I didn't open them."

"Why not?"

"I believe she is talking to Ivor and other people who would like to see me behind bars," Park responded.

Webster quizzed Park on his delay to return from France after his wife's body had been found.

"You had felt for 20 years or more that your wife had betrayed you," Webster put it to Park. "Then on holiday in France you get the appalling news that she had not betrayed you but had been murdered. Yet you didn't return to England?"

"Yes."

When Park admitted not contacting the police, Webster said, "You put her in the lake."

"No."

"What you needed at that point in France was time to think, to get your thoughts together before you faced the police," Webster stated.

"No," shot back Park, "I couldn't get home any sooner."

Webster then asked Park why he had sold his boat on Coniston and handed him a copy of his own logbook. He asked Park when he had sold it.

Park took the copy of the document, and answered, "I believe it was June 1976."

Webster said, "But you wrote in your own logbook in your own writing that it was July 1976."

Park stared at Webster, then replied: "I don't know why I put that. It was definitely June."

Park became annoyed when Webster suggested he had had the opportunity to murder Carol if he'd wanted to. Park gripped the sides of the witness box and had to concede this was true but insisted that such a suggestion was absurd.

Webster put it to Park that he alone would have had access to his wife in her nightie – the attire in which her body was discovered – and was also proficient in tying knots and had the use of a boat. He also fitted the description of a man seen dropping a heavy package into the lake.

Webster said Park could also have easily hidden the body, "You had somewhere to put her and work out what you were going to do. You had a chest freezer?"

A rattled Park replied, "Yes. We had a chest freezer, and if I'd wanted to do it I would have had the opportunity. Yes."

Webster said, "You had to swallow your pride on a number of occasions when she returned having been with other men."

Park's anger was barely disguised. He replied, "I did not have a motive for killing Carol. She was my wife and the mother of my children. I loved her. It is absurd to suggest I would kill her."

Webster pressed on, "Was it humiliating to find out she was having more affairs around that time?"

Park replied, "I've heard since that this was the case."

"She hurt you once too often, didn't she, Mr Park?"

Park said this wasn't the case.

"You'd had enough, hadn't you, Mr Park? You had taken her back time and time again."

Park interrupted the barrister sharply, "If you knew this girl you would also have forgiven her."

"Just as weaved-together strings of a rope," Webster said, "you have been weaving together strings of fact and fiction during the evidence, haven't you?"

"No."

It was an electric exchange. The brilliance of Alistair Webster's cross-examination had shaken Park's signature surface cool.

The defendant stepped down from the witness box.

32

Beyond Sensible Doubt

In the coming days, Andrew Edis would call upon the rest of the 12 witnesses.

Jenny Park stepped into the witness box, her husband sitting feet away in the dock. She described the man she had known for most of her life and to whom she had been married for 11 years. She said in all their time together he had never been a violent person and had never made any confession to her about killing Carol.

Smiling at the judge, she said, "He is kind, compassionate, gentle. I'm very frightened of large spiders and he will always catch the spider and remove it. He wouldn't kill it."

Edis questioned the defence team's own experts on the police's evidence, including the knots and lead piping. Dr Kenneth Pye gave his views on the rock recovered from the lake.

Junior defence counsel Brian Williams read out a statement from Carlisle-based judge Barbara Forrester, who had been

Park's solicitor at the time of his first arrest in 1997. In it she detailed the circumstances around Park's interview with the *Mail on Sunday* for which he was paid £50,000. Forrester said the decision to do the interview had come on her advice because of the intense media scrutiny Park and Jenny were under in 1997 after his arrest and subsequently in 1998 after the murder charge was dropped.

She said all the national newspapers had sent reporters to Barrow and had requested interviews with Park. Things came to a head when a reporter stole a wedding photo of Park and Jenny from their conservatory at Norland Avenue. The Parks later complained to the regulator of the Press Complaints Commission and received an apology.

After the murder charge was dropped in 1998, the Parks went into hiding. There was huge demand for Park's story. He felt that if his privacy was being compromised he might as well get something out of it, so Forrester approached a retired Fleet Street freelance reporter. His advice was that if Park sold his story he should retain editorial control. They received offers of £50,000 from the *News of the World* and the *Mail on Sunday* and Park chose the latter as he preferred it as a newspaper.

In her statement to the court, Forrester said that once the payment was made, Park gave £10,000 to the Lake District freelance journalist who wrote the story, and £2,500 to Ms Forrester. That left Park with £37,500 to cover costs he'd incurred at the time of his arrest.

In concluding the case for the defence, Andrew Edis had reserved a counterpunch to all the circumstantial evidence put forward by the police and the Crown Prosecution Service.

He asserted that none of this evidence pointed directly to

Gordon Park, which left open the possibility that somebody else might have killed Carol, a possibility that could include John Rapson, the murderer of Carol's sister Christine, who was being allowed out of prison each weekend in 1976. Edis suggested Rapson might have gone to Leece in search of his daughter Vanessa and during an argument killed Carol on 17 July.

By the third week of January the Crown and defence barristers prepared to give their closing remarks to the jury. This was the opportunity for Webster and Edis to leave the jury with very different portraits of the man in the dock.

Webster stood and delivered a devastating demolition of Park's public reputation. He branded the retired schoolteacher as a cold-blooded and calculated killer. A methodical man, Park had most likely murdered his wife Carol and hidden her body in the chest freezer while he worked out how he was going to dispose of it.

There was only one verdict open to the jury, Webster insisted.

"What we have here is a clear pattern," he said. Pointing to the overwhelming circumstantial evidence, he said it all added up to "a template of a killer, and it fits Gordon Park perfectly."

He said Park had shown his true colours in a court of law before, "when he wanted custody of his children, he lied under oath."

And he said Park had selected the perfect day on which to kill his wife. "What would be the best day of the year to kill a teacher if you were planning to stall as long as possible any investigation into her disappearance?

"It would be the first day of the summer holidays, the very day she disappeared," he explained.

He poured scorn on claims another man had killed Carol

and asked, "Is this consistent with some passing burglar or homicidal lover, or does it show the killer was acting in a calculating manner?"

Had an intruder killed Carol, Webster suggested, he would have sought a quick and discreet escape. It was implausible he would dispose of the body in the manner it had been. As it was, the injuries to the body were an attempt to conceal the identity, as was the removal of her engagement and wedding ring which was inscribed with the date of her marriage.

"We say this was a form of insurance for the killer."

Webster looked directly at the jury and said, "He did kill Carol Park and there is no room for any sensible doubt."

It was a brilliant performance. The jury were processing Webster's words. Gordon Park remained silent in the dock. Reporters scratched the final words into their notebooks, ready to file their copy of the day's events.

The following day Andrew Edis made his closing remarks for the defence. He had a word of warning for the jury. "You are not Miss Marple or Hercule Poirot. You are not here to solve the puzzle, you're here to return a verdict.

"Of course, what you'd like to do is solve the puzzle. You would like to say at the end of the case, 'I know what happened' because in a way that's what it's like in detective stories and in some cases this may resemble a detective story. What we haven't got is Miss Marple or Mr Poirot to solve the puzzle and to come in now and say 'we will explain'. What we've got is the evidence and your own judgement about it."

He warned the jury about the fallibility of memory over time.

"In the end nobody saw [Park] do this," Edis said. "Nobody heard him do it. There was no blood, hair or anything else from Carol Park found at home or on him, which would prove murder."

The only certainty, Edis instructed the jury, was that Carol Park had died a violent death.

He reiterated his point that Carol might have been murdered by the same man who killed her sister: John Rapson. Given Rapson's conviction for violent sexual offences and predilection for bondage, Edis mooted, he was a plausible suspect especially as it could have been possible he was in the Barrow area on 17 July 1976. According to Edis, Rapson was on probation after being released from prison and saw his probation officer on 29 July where Rapson said he'd been granted two weeks' leave, although there were no prison records to confirm this.

Edis hypothesised that Rapson might have driven to Bluestones in a VW Beetle car that had been spotted outside the Parks' home at the time of Carol's disappearance.

Edis admitted it was difficult to see how Rapson might have killed Carol but added, "Remember that what we are putting before you are other pieces of evidence which show other possible exercises in relation to the killing of Carol Park."

In his closing remarks, Edis told jurors, "Members of the jury, when did he kill the woman that he loved? Nobody has been able to tell you that. Unless you can answer that question you have to have doubt about whether he killed Carol Park.

"All we ask you to do is judge him on the evidence."

And so the trial was approaching its climax. All the preparation, the financial, intellectual and emotional cost had been in service of this one purpose: determining the guilt or otherwise of Gordon Park.

The members of the jury must have been overwhelmed by

everything they had heard. On the morning of Wednesday, 26 January 2005, it was time for the judge, the Honourable Mr Justice McCombe to sum up the case.

He thanked the jury for their concentration which, he told them, he had watched with admiration and gratitude. He would give them direction on how they should reach their verdict. He would do this by highlighting the prominent features of the evidence as they occurred to him.

"However," he told them, "it is your task and your responsibility to judge that evidence and decide all the relevant facts. When you come to consider your verdict, you and you alone do that."

And so he spent the whole of Wednesday and part of Thursday summarising the case and, as he promised, highlighting the elements of the evidence he felt were significant. It was a long, protracted process and McCombe adjourned the court at various points during the two days to give the jury a break.

He told the jurors to discount the fact Park had sold his story to the newspapers. That, he said, was irrelevant.

After hours of speaking, McCombe reached his conclusion after lunch on Thursday. It was time for the jury to go away and make their deliberations. He reminded them they must reach, if they could, a unanimous verdict. If this were not possible then, in certain circumstances, a majority verdict might be acceptable.

"Ladies and gentlemen," he instructed them, "would you go with the ushers, and they will take you to your room."

Waiting for them were the exhibits from the case should they wish to review them further. The time was 12.30pm.

Everybody in the courtroom rose to their feet and the judge

retired to his quarters. The tension was instantly released. The public gallery and the press bench broke into chatter. Gordon Park stepped down from the dock, no doubt anxious at what lay ahead. The legal teams gathered papers and swapped comments before vacating the courtroom to stretch their legs.

There was nothing more to be done other than wait.

How long a jury takes to reach its verdict is impossible to determine. During that Thursday afternoon, the jury returned to the courtroom on a couple of occasions to ask specific questions of the judge. Such breaks in a jury's deliberations are not swift interludes: they require the judge, jury, prosecution and defence counsel and the defendant to return to the courtroom. It is like a resetting of a theatre scene ready for a performance to restart. Reporters, too, rush back with their pens poised in case it is a moment of significance.

Finally, at just before 4.20pm on Thursday, McCombe called back the jury. It had been a long day. He thanked them for the deliberations so far but said he was sending them home for the evening. But he gave them a warning, "It is important that after you leave the court, you should not discuss the case with anyone else or allow anyone else to speak to you."

On a lighter note, he urged them, "Just go home, enjoy a quiet evening and come back refreshed and ready for work tomorrow again, please."

33

The Verdict

The following morning, Friday, 28 January, just like all the other mornings since November, Manchester Crown Court was filled with barristers, witnesses, journalists and members of the public. Gordon Park stepped into the dock. On the dot of 10am, the judge, the Honourable Mr Justice McCombe, instructed the jury to continue their deliberations. They rose to their feet and left for the jury room.

Everyone waited.

During the recess, Park sat with his wife Jenny in the waiting area outside Court 4. They were engrossed in a crossword puzzle to distract them. At one point, Jenny Park broke off from the diversion to tell *Westmorland Gazette* reporter Jennie Dennett that her husband was confident he would be acquitted.

"He does not believe they can convict him on the evidence they have," she said. Park sat at her side, a pen poised over the puzzle. The wait continued for the solution to the bigger puzzle under scrutiny in the jury room.

The day before, Park had thanked a reporter from the *North*

West Evening Mail for what he considered was unbiased and truthful coverage of the trial. He told the reporter it had been nice to see a friendly face each day. As he might not get the chance again, he wished to pass on his thanks to the paper's journalists. He promised that if he were acquitted he would speak exclusively to the local newspapers in Cumbria about his 28-year nightmare.

The *Evening Mail* reporter asked how he was feeling as he awaited the verdict.

Park replied, "To be honest I feel like I am on another planet."

DS Doug Marshall was unsurprised by Park's courting of the media. He'd seen the same peacocking in 1998 after the first murder charge was dropped. Park's response was to give an interview to the *Mail on Sunday* for £50,000.

Marshall said, "You know, most of us, if we were in court for a very serious crime, we wouldn't necessarily be planning our interview strategy. You'd be more focused on the trial and making sure you cleared your name if you're innocent."

He recalled Park's arrogance ahead of the verdict, "I don't think he thought he was going to get found guilty. I think he had got it into his head that he had done enough to cool everyone and get himself off."

It was a tense time for the detectives. Marshall recalled, "There was never a time when I felt certain he was going to be found guilty. In terms of suspense it's probably the biggest moment in my life. I could feel my heart beating hard."

DI Huddleston remembered, "The atmosphere in the court was so tense. I don't think I've ever been in court with a tense atmosphere like that. It was electric."

After seven long hours, Park was called back, along with the lawyers, the police, the families, the reporters and those in the public gallery.

The jury had reached a verdict.

Prior to the jury's return, Judge McCombe sounded a warning, "For the benefit of all in court, I ask that when the verdict is delivered, that everybody behaves with dignity and observes complete silence. It is a difficult moment for very many people."

Sitting in the gallery, intermingled with the press, were Ivor Price and his family, Park's wife Jenny and Jeremy and Rachael. During the trial the Parks and Prices had sat at opposite ends of the public gallery and kept their distance in the waiting areas outside Court 4.

The judge turned to the ushers and said, "Thank you. The jury, please."

The court fell silent. One by one, each juror returned and took his or her seat. The only noise was the shuffling of feet and the occasional cough.

Once the jury was settled, the clerk of the court rose and asked, "Will the foreman please stand?"

A woman on the jury rose to her feet.

"Madam Foreman," the clerk continued, "will you please answer my first question yes or no. Have the jury reached a verdict upon which you are all agreed?"

Absolute silence in court; absolute tension.

"Yes," replied the woman foreman.

"Do you find the defendant Gordon Park guilty or not guilty of murder?"

Silence.

The woman foreman, the fate of Park in her hands, spoke.

A single word, one that reverberated around the courtroom. "Guilty."

There were gasps, audible and silent.

"You find the defendant guilty?" asked the clerk, seeking confirmation. "And that is the verdict of you all?"

"Yes," said the woman foreman, sealing Gordon Park's fate in a single breath.

Park shut his eyes, slumped forward in the dock and put his head in one hand. Jenny gave a terrible shriek from the gallery and burst into tears. She was holding a white handkerchief.

"Thank you," said the clerk of the court, who then instructed the jurors to sit down, before turning to Park in the dock.

"Sit down, Mr Park," the clerk said.

The judge turned to Park to sentence him. Accepting there were mitigating circumstances, he said, "Gordon Park, for this offence of murder the sentence is imprisonment for life. I sentence you to life. The time you have to serve before you are considered for release is 15 years. That does not mean you will be released. That will be decided by us."

The judge had taken into account the brutality of the attack and the subsequent suffering caused to the family. The terrible concealment of the body was another aggravating factor.

Park was in a trance. He grasped the rail in front of him for support. He appeared confused as the realisation sank in: the justice system had caught up with him. Security guards appeared at his side. They led him like a zombie down to the cells.

Ivor Price, the man who had faithfully fought for justice for his sister, fainted in the public gallery when he heard the word 'guilty'. The release of 30 years of worry and uncertainty was all too much.

He later said of the moment, "Tremendous shock. They say I collapsed. I did. I don't know much about that, it was seconds. Then I felt a numbness and then I just felt, well, it's justice for Carol and that's what this has been about."

Jeremy Park was stunned. He looked shell-shocked, reporters later remembered. His sister Rachael turned to her husband and sobbed into his shoulder. The Parks were in tears as they left the courtroom. Jeremy told reporters, "Please just leave us alone."

DS Marshall was unsurprised by Park's reaction to the verdict, "I'm sure for him it would be disbelief because I'm sure he was arrogant to the point of thinking he was going to get away with it."

For the detectives it was vindication of years of hard, intensive work.

"There was no euphoria from my team," said DCI Keith Churchman. "We weren't punching the air and shouting and cheering because there were too many victims in this case, you know. Carol Park's family, victims then and victims now, and victims forever."

DS Marshall told reporters the verdict brought to an end years of wondering what had happened to Carol Park.

"The jury affirmed that Gordon Park was the killer, something which I had believed all along," he said, reflecting on his disappointment that there hadn't been a conviction in 1997.

"We never gave up on the case which is how we have arrived at the situation we are in. Persistence has paid off," he said.

DI Geoff Huddleston told journalists, "Ivor Price has waited a long time for the case to come to trial. It was tense this afternoon. Without any doubt we got the right man."

Reporters and TV crews waited outside the court. They wanted the reactions of the police, lawyers and families.

A recovered Ivor Price emerged into the January chill to speak to the media. With decades of worry etched into his face, he spoke eloquently and with his characteristic fairness.

He said, "Today is about one thing, justice for Carol and peace for my mother who died from a broken heart."

He became emotional but continued, "Her last words to me were 'find Carol' and we did."

A man not given to rancour or bitterness, Ivor nevertheless could not hold back his feelings of contempt for Gordon Park. He branded his brother-in-law a "habitual liar" and told reporters, "To say he is a human being is to say the wrong thing. I just think he is a very evil character."

At a press conference after the verdict, DS Doug Marshall said, "Early alarm bells were ringing particularly when we found out Park hadn't reported his wife missing for six weeks and only then through a solicitor."

DI Geoff Huddleston outlined the police's theory of what Park had done to Carol on that fateful day in July 1976. They believed Park had sedated her with the antidepressant Triptisol before smashing her face with an axe. It was thought Park had bound her body in a foetal position using a suite of complex sailing knots, before putting it into bin bags and a makeshift shroud using a rucksack and a pinafore dress of Carol's. Huddlestone said police believed Park hid her body in the family's chest freezer and attached sticking plasters over her eyes to hide her lifeless stare.

DCI Keith Churchman told reporters, "Whether he did it during a fit of temper or a cold calculated murder, we can't be sure. Hopefully one day he will tell us so the family and friends can know what happened to her." He revealed that Park's arrogance in police interviews had extended to goading detectives to prove he had killed his wife.

Detectives believed Park's later interest in Buddhism was the act of a murderer trying to assuage a guilty conscience.

News of Park's conviction came as a huge shock to his neighbours on Norland Avenue back home in Barrow. David and Hazel Wheeler, who had known their neighbour for eight years, had expected to see Park back home, a free man. "When I heard the verdict I was shocked," Hazel Wheeler told the *Evening Mail*. "There was no evidence against him. It's a travesty of justice." David Wheeler said Park was a popular figure in the area.

Another Norland Avenue resident, Bob Gelling, felt sorry for Park because he didn't think there was enough evidence to convict him.

The guilty verdict, however, confirmed what many people in the wider Leece and Barrow community had long been thinking: Gordon Park had murdered his wife.

Bill Lawson, the original policeman who investigated Carol's disappearance in 1976, said. "That poor lass, all these years people thought she'd gone off with somebody and all these years she's been lying there and he's got away with it."

Anne Walker, who had felt a maternal duty to Carol when she had stayed at the High Duddon Guest House, said, "If he'd admitted what he'd done 30 years ago he'd have served a shorter sentence, he'd have been out and it would all have been over and done with sooner than this. So, I'm sorry, if he's going to spend 20 years at the end of his life then it's only what he deserves."

Gordon Park, now aged 61, was on his way to Manchester Prison in the Strangeways district of the city.

There was barely a second to breathe for the detectives. After the press conference ended, it was time to return to Cumbria. They would need to go through the exhibits from the trial, items to be returned to families. It would be a period of decompression.

DCI Churchman nominated his team for the Chief Constable's Commendation. The detectives were honoured at a special presentation event on 21 December 2005 and were featured in local press coverage.

Marshall received the highest honour as he was the officer who had bridged the two investigations. The citation read: "Detective Sergeant Marshall is commended for his diligence, dedication and immense persistence throughout the 'Lady in the Lake' investigation being the only officer involved from the start of the inquiry when the body was discovered in Coniston Water in July 1997 through to the eventual conviction of the murderer in 2005. After the victim's husband was released due to lack of evidence, Detective Sergeant Marshall continued to investigate the murder. His perseverance resulted in new evidence being discovered which reinvigorated the investigation."

Marshall reflected on the honour, "It's important to mark good work, particularly when people go above and beyond and have worked hundreds and hundreds of hours, a lot of it your own time that you don't get paid for. It's a quest, it's a challenge."

To this day he believes the justice detectives delivered for Carol and the peace they brought to the Price family were the detectives' biggest rewards.

Shortly after the verdict, Park's solicitor Mike Graham issued a statement to say the family was devastated. Park was concerned not for himself, the statement read, but for his family: his children had lost their mother and now were faced with the tragedy of their father's conviction.

Now the legal team were considering whether there were grounds for an appeal. The fight to clear Park's name was certainly not over.

"It is not in the stars to hold our destiny but in ourselves."

— William Shakespeare

PART FOUR

THE AFTERMATH

34

Prison Writings

It was January 2005 and I was sitting in a poky newspaper office in an industrial town on the banks of the Mersey in Cheshire. Three weeks earlier I'd been appointed Editor of the *Runcorn and Widnes World*. I shared the cramped upstairs newsroom with three reporters, one sub-editor and an editorial assistant.

Naturally, I had been following the Park trial across all the newspapers with great interest but I'd been most focused on the *Westmorland Gazette*'s coverage. On a recent trip to Kendal, I'd taken my wife and young daughter to the *Gazette* office to see old colleagues. There were many familiar faces still there, including Mike Addison and Andrew Thomas, complemented by younger journalists new to the team since I'd left.

One was Jennie Dennett. She'd covered the entire seven weeks of Park's trial. Her report of the verdict was published on Friday, 4 February. The main headline read: 'After three decades the mystery is finally solved: As Gordon Park begins a life sentence for the 'Lady in the Lake' murder, reporter Jennie Dennett looks back to when his wife's body was rediscovered in

Coniston Water in 1997 and remembers a young life that was so cruelly cut short'.

She interviewed diver David Mason. Now, almost eight years on, he reflected on the impact of their discovery of the body. Speaking at home in Kendal, he told Dennett the knowledge of their mother's death had enabled the Park children to bury her, but it might have been better for them to live in hope by not knowing.

The discovery had not immediately affected Mason. It was only after Carol Park was identified that it tormented his thoughts. He tried to forget what he'd seen but each time the case returned to the public eye it dredged up dark memories. As a father himself, he was troubled by thoughts of the Park children losing their mother and now seeing their father convicted of her murder.

Dennett explored this strand in a moving breakout story. She described the impact on the children as the "biggest tragedy". She wrote that Vanessa had chosen to stay out of the limelight because of trauma. Vanessa was a "talented horse whisperer" who "now takes comfort in being around horses". Her uncle, Ivor Price told Dennett he was "disgusted" with Park for instructing his legal team to suggest Carol might have been murdered by John Rapson, the man who murdered Vanessa's birth mother. How could he do that to his own daughter, he asked.

As a follow-up idea, Jennie Dennett contacted Gordon Park. She sent a letter to Prisoner NV5678 at Manchester Prison. She included a series of questions about his thoughts and how he was passing his time while serving a 15-year sentence. It was a vain hope because Park had refused all requests for interviews.

But one day in October she was shocked to receive a reply. Park said he was happy to grant her a "written interview". It was certainly a journalistic coup and made for an eye-catching story in the *Gazette*.

In a piece that milked every drop of drama from the letter, Dennett wrote that Park clung to hope of persuading the world of his innocence. He confided that his mind "was still in turmoil" since being found guilty.

Park wrote that he had given direct answers to questions in court, believing that the truth would "speak for itself". The jury, it seemed, did not believe him.

That was as much as Park would discuss about the case, the trial and the murder of Carol. The remainder of the letter was dedicated to describing his discomfort at being behind bars. He described his 13-foot by six-foot prison cell from where he wrote the letter, sitting at his Formica desk. The cell had the "luxury" of a plug, a television set and an adjacent room with a flushing toilet and hand basin. His cell had a window, although a flap denied him a view outside. It was exactly as you'd imagine, he wrote, the cell redolent of prison-based television programmes Porridge and Bad Girls. He was writing to her from his sixth such cell, he told Dennett, and had "an agreeable cell-mate".

Being cooped up for hour after hour was torture, explained Park, who had been used to an active life walking, climbing and sailing in the Lake District. He had to be content with scenic pictures of the Lake District, Walney Island, Dalton-in-Furness and Yorkshire secured to his cell notice board with sticky tape salvaged from prisoners' lunchtime sandwich wrappers. Drawing pins were banned as they could be misused violently.

Park was critical of the regime at Manchester Prison and concessions given to prisoners. He claimed he and other inmates might be "banged up" in their cells all day if prison officers failed to come in to work or if it was a bank holiday. He decried the "outrageous" 10p-a-minute phone calls, limiting his conversations with Jenny.

With so much time on his hands, Park had to find ways to occupy his mind. He was working in the prison library and in the information technology workshop, earning a prison salary of £5.45 a week. He was also studying contemporary politics.

He praised the prison's chaplaincy who were supporting him. As a committed churchgoer, he was attending a Church of England service every Sunday morning. He found the singing of the other prisoners during the service moving.

Every day he would write a long letter to Jenny expressing his concerns about other prisoners. Prison-life was unnerving and he had witnessed many disturbing scenes. He was scared by the stealing and lying of the inmates and had seen one taking drugs and 'chasing the dragon'.

Park declined to tell Dennett whether he was writing his autobiography. A manuscript had been alluded to during Park's trial and Dennett was curious to know more.

In her piece, she outlined the developments unfolding beyond the thick walls of Manchester Prison. ITV was making a television documentary as part of its Real Crime strand, but she noted the programme-makers would not be sympathetic to Park's claims to be an innocent victim of a miscarriage of justice.

She reported that Jeremy and Rachael refused to believe their father had killed their mother and had begun a campaign, 'Free Gordon', to see him cleared and released from prison.

They hoped another television documentary might be made exposing their father's wrongful conviction.

Dennett concluded her piece with this thought: it was doubtful that Park would ever return to Cumbria as a free man.

She had no further letters from Park.

35

Free Gordon

As Park adjusted to life at Manchester Prison, his spirits were lifted by regular visits by Jenny and Jeremy. He didn't discuss the case much; he was in shock and reliving the trial was too much. Instead, Jeremy recalled, he would try to lift their spirits by making jokes and laughing with them. "That must have been hard for him," Jeremy remembered. "Sometimes you could see he was just numb with boredom, frustration and anger. It was just heartbreaking, and sometimes you came out of there sobbing."

Jeremy set up a website to support the campaign to clear his father's name. The front page of FreeGordon.com was headed with a bold statement: 'Another Travesty of Justice has Occurred'. There followed a brief summary of the case for unfamiliar readers. It was a whistle-stop trip through three heart-wrenching decades. Gordon Park, Jeremy wrote, "is now serving a 15 year life sentence".

Jeremy laid out their arguments, stating that Park's family and friends believed he was innocent and the evidence during the trial was "so poor that it could match any number of people".

In their view, there was no evidence connecting Park to the crime and it was their belief "the burden of proof has not been discharged in this case [...] We will fight for justice for as long as is necessary."

In 2006, Jeremy spoke to the local ITV news programme, *Granada Reports*, about the campaign. "We don't trust the police," he said. "But in terms of what's important, I just want to know who killed my Mum and I'd like my Dad to come out of prison."

He set up a petition addressed to the UK Government on the website PetitionOnline.com with the statement: "We believe the murder conviction of Gordon Park to be unsafe and support the campaign to appeal against his conviction. Sincerely, The Undersigned." (When I accessed the petition in December 2023 – 18 years after it was set up – there were 167 signatures.)

Inside the website were many pages picking over the case in great detail. There was a separate page dedicated to each of the key pieces of evidence that convicted Park: the 1976 missing person's inquiry, the knots, the rock, the lead piping, Park's boats and the purported prison cell confessions of Park. There was also a transcript of the judge's summing up at the trial.

The website made strong criticisms of allegations made in a national newspaper that Park and a senior police officer destroyed the 1976 missing persons report because both were Freemasons. In reality, the website said, Park had never been a Freemason and this spurious claim emerged only after the trial. If it were true, "at the very least, this is tantamount to an admission of police corruption".

FreeGordon.com examined Carol's and Park's characters. Carol had a tendency to walk out of the family home without warning for short periods of time. During her marriage to Park she had had several relationships with other men – including a police officer (this was probably Brearley) and a solicitor. In each case she had ultimately left these lovers suddenly and was welcomed back to Bluestones by Park. She timed her dalliances with the start and end of the school holidays. This implied that when she disappeared in 1976, Park was conditioned to believe she would return in time for the new school year in September 1976. When she didn't, Park notified Ivor Price and his solicitor.

The website contended that Gordon Park had been the victim of a character assassination during the police investigation and subsequent trial. He had been portrayed as a "cold, calculating and violent killer who had lied to his family and was continuing to do so by not admitting his guilt", and was a disciplinarian who beat his children. The website claimed this was the opposite of the truth. Park's true character had been shown in the defence testimonies of his children and step-children and of his lifelong friends – some stretching back 50 years. Not one person had ever seen Park be violent. He had no previous convictions and had won custody of Vanessa, Jeremy and Rachael all those years earlier when Carol had gone to live with David Brearley. "It was highly unusual during the 1970s, as now, for men to be awarded custody," the website said, "and this was therefore a vindication of Gordon's good character and his capability as a parent."

Jeremy, Rachael and Jenny poured their hearts into the FreeGordon campaign, their pain seared into every word. Reading it today, it is difficult to imagine the suffering they endured.

In 2006, Jeremy Park told a reporter, "If I thought my dad

had killed my mum, I would let him rot in that prison. But that's not the truth. We're dealing here with a terrible miscarriage of justice. My mum is the obvious victim – she's dead. But my dad has become another victim. He's locked up every day for a crime he didn't commit – and we can't allow that to happen."

The FreeGordon petition received high-profile support in the shape of Labour Party politician Tony Benn, a famously vocal supporter of underdog causes. Former Chesterfield and Bristol South East MP Benn said he had read lots of letters detailing the case and evidence used to convict Park and believed there was sufficient doubt over the conviction.

He said, "As a result I feel this is a miscarriage of justice and so am fully supporting this campaign and will do all I can to help."

For many observers, however, the question burned: how could his children stand by Park when everyone else was convinced he murdered Carol?

Detective Sergeant Doug Marshall said, "You will get people who will say 'Oh my God, how could they stand by him? The murdering blah blah blah. But it's a really difficult thing for a family and my heart still goes out to the children because whether you agree with the decision they made or you don't, it's irrelevant. It was a terrible thing for them that the mother disappeared. The father's saying it wasn't him and the police are saying it is. And there's no middle ground.

"You have to come down on one side and they did decide at that stage to support the father."

Inevitably, this put a wedge between the police and the Park children, making it difficult to offer the support normally given to families. "It made communication very difficult," said Marshall.

One of Park's most vocal supporters was Pastor George Harrison, the minister of Pendlebury Evangelical Church in Swinton, Greater Manchester, with whom Park stayed during the trial. He made regular visits from Pendlebury to offer pastoral support to the imprisoned Park at Strangeways, a distance of under two miles. During these visits, Harrison was impressed by Park's caring and gentle nature and became convinced of his innocence. He was also dubious of the evidence that convicted Park. In sympathy with the FreeGordon petition, Harrison stepped up his crusade with an evangelical zeal. On the first anniversary of Park's incarceration, he led a number of Park's supporters, including Jenny and Jeremy, in a vigil outside the prison.

In September 2007, Park was transferred north from Manchester Prison to HMP Garth in Leyland, Lancashire. Pastor Harrison was no longer allowed to visit Park here, a claim he made later in an interview with the *Manchester Evening News*. He alleged it was prison bosses who imposed the ban, blaming their unhappiness with the prayer vigils he had led and his criticism of Cumbria Police in their dealing of Park. The *Manchester Evening News* put Harrison's allegations to the Ministry of Justice, which issued a statement to the effect that each prison retained faith representatives "to ensure that prisoners have every opportunity to practise their religion". The implication was that Park would be visited by HMP Garth's own ministry team.

The transfer to a new prison and the severing of contact with Harrison sent Park into a spiral of depression.

Media interest in the Lady in the Lake case was usually predicated on the assumption Gordon Park was guilty. But ·

as the FreeGordon movement gained traction, support came from the author of a book about injustice. In 2008, three years after Park was incarcerated, *No Smoke! The Shocking Truth About British Justice* was published. Each chapter featured a British criminal case the author considered to be a wrongful conviction. She blamed flawed evidence and conclusions reached by the courts.

One chapter was dedicated to Gordon Park.

The author of the book was Sandra Lean who, by her own admission, had a deep interest in the workings of the criminal mind. At the age of 32 she had studied for a degree in psychology and sociology at Edinburgh's Napier University before taking a master's degree in forensic psychology. At the time she was working on *No Smoke* she was studying for her doctorate in criminal justice at the University of Stirling.

In the blurb to her book, Lean wrote, "Innocent people are being locked up in our prisons, convicted of the most horrific crimes, on a regular basis. These are not one-off, tragic mistakes, but rather, a routine everyday occurrence.

"For every high-profile miscarriage of justice that we hear about, there are dozens more that never make the news."

This latter point did not apply to Gordon Park, of course. His case had been scrutinised in great detail by the media for the best part of 11 years when Lean published her book. Nevertheless, she was convinced Park was an innocent man.

Lean criticised Park's trial and conviction in a lengthy series of points. There was no DNA evidence linking him to the murder; instead the conviction was based purely on circumstantial evidence. In her view, there had been an over-reliance on expert testimony, while Park's unblemished reputation had been destroyed by witnesses with vested interests in seeing him go down.

She argued that police files had been inconsistently and poorly recorded. She believed the case had not been proved beyond all reasonable doubt, the threshold a jury must reach in making its decision to convict.

The book riled the police and prosecutors on the case. When I interviewed detective Doug Marshall in early 2023 he bristled when I mentioned Lean's book. The book also angered Dick Binstead of the Crown Prosecution Service. He would take up his pen years later to counter Lean's claims and write his own memoir about the case.

In July 2008, Park made an unusual request of Jenny. He asked her to send him the official report into the death of Harold Shipman, the serial killer GP from Greater Manchester, who had taken his own life in prison in 2004. Park never told her why he wanted the report by the Prisons and Probation Ombudsman; she never asked. And so she acquired a copy and sent it to him. In the report it detailed how Shipman, who had been convicted in 2000 of murdering 15 of his patients, (his victims are thought to run into the hundreds) had committed suicide by hanging while serving a life sentence at HMP Wakefield.

Jenny was concerned about Park's spirits. He was very low but was pinning hopes on a successful appeal against his conviction.

Meanwhile, Park had appointed a new legal team, Clarion solicitors in Leeds, who were mounting the appeal they claimed was based on fresh evidence not available at Park's trial. In a statement, Clarion – which was working with barrister Simon

Bourne-Arton QC – had formally lodged Grounds of Appeal against his murder conviction. "It is hoped the conviction will be quashed and a retrial ordered," a media statement from Clarion read. Park had no automatic right of appeal against his Crown Court conviction. Instead, his legal team had to seek permission – known as leave to appeal – to allow the appeal to be heard.

The announcement prompted a statement in December 2007 from Cumbria Police, which stated, "Detectives from Cumbria Constabulary carried out a full and thorough investigation and the full facts of the case were presented to the CPS. The case was then tried by a jury, where Gordon Park was found guilty of the murder of Carol Park in 1976."

When the bid to win leave to appeal was heard at the Appeal Court in London on Thursday, 27 November 2008, Park's barrister Simon Bourne-Arton revealed that an expert in geology would challenge the evidence at Park's trial relating to the rock said to have been used to weigh down the body and to be indistinguishable from samples taken from Bluestones. A new expert would show the rock was actually "indistinguishable" from other rocks found widely in the Coniston area. Jeremy and Jenny listened in court, hopeful the judges would be swayed by the new evidence and order a retrial.

The judges listened to the new evidence but in the end they felt that the rock had formed only one part of a strong circumstantial case against Park. They told Bourne-Arton this was not enough to allow an appeal against conviction.

Sixty-four-year-old Park was sitting in his cell at Garth Prison in Lancashire nervously awaiting news of the hearing. His future depended on a retrial, an opportunity to convince a jury he was not guilty. His shell-shocked supporters spilled out of the courts onto the Strand. Jenny telephoned her husband with news of the judgement. As she spoke, Park broke down, his sobs pouring down the line.

"It was a really horrible moment," said Jeremy. "It absolutely crushed him."

36

A Broken Man

Park found conditions at Garth Prison worse than Manchester. Family visits at Strangeways had been straightforward but Garth was a different set-up altogether.

On a rare trip home from China, Rachael endured being searched for drugs by a sniffer dog and when she sat down with her father she was shocked when she was denied physical contact with him. A glass screen separated them and they sat at opposite ends of a long counter-top. She could barely hear what he was saying because of the constant banging of prison doors, while the room's acoustics made it almost impossible to hold a coherent conversation. The final indignity, Rachael later recalled, was the brevity of the time they were allowed together.

Jeremy Park watched his father become ground down by prison life. Park had taught him to be resilient and independent, to take command of his own life, but now Jeremy could only look on and watch as his father lost his liberty and finally his spirit. There was nothing he could do.

"By the end, he was like Job," said Jeremy, "railing against the injustices he'd suffered."

Alone in his cell, Park would put on music, lie on his bed and listen to the songs he no doubt had played on guitar at home in Norland Avenue. And his mind would wander, transporting him to the open fells of the Lake District, imagining the musical notes were the songs of birds as they circled over the lakes and mountains.

He was 65 years old and there was nothing on the horizon to give him hope of ever walking free from prison. On Sunday, 24 January 2010, Jenny spoke to Park on the phone as she usually did. The following day would be his 66th birthday and she wanted to lift his spirits, but she found her husband in a desperate state. As she tried to speak to him all she could hear was him crying. He was a broken man. The phone call ended.

There was nothing she could do.

Early on Monday, 25 January, prison officers were waking prisoners and making their daily checks. It was 8am when they entered Gordon Park's cell and found him unconscious with a ligature around his neck. Paramedics were called and found him unresponsive. They tried to resuscitate him but by 9.40am the decision was taken to pronounce him dead. It was clear Park had taken his own life.

He was 66 to the day.

After Park's family were notified, news of his death was announced to the media. Once more the case of the Lady in the Lake was back in the headlines, 34 years after Carol Park had gone missing. Once more, the Parks' son Jeremy found himself in the media spotlight. He gave a statement to journalists, "We are all completely devastated and still believe his innocence 100 per cent."

DS Doug Marshall remembers hearing the news. He said, "It wasn't a day of rejoicing. It was just another sad epitaph to an already very sad case because not only have the family lost a mother, now their father's dead. I just remember feeling a bit empty."

It would be more than three years before the inquest into Park's death. It was heard in Preston before a jury and in front of coroner Dr James Adeley in March 2013. Park's widow Jenny gave evidence and told the hearing of her husband's request for the report into the suicide of Dr Harold Shipman. She explained how she'd sent it to him but hadn't known what he wanted with it. She explained that he had made the request in the summer of 2008, four months before his application for leave to appeal, a hearing he had pinned all his hopes on. When this had failed, she said, he became depressed.

The coroner asked how he changed.

"In his whole demeanour," she replied.

He had found it hard when visits by Pastor Harrison stopped without satisfactory explanation. The failed appeal bid had been the final blow. She said it was "something else that had happened to him that he had no control over".

The inquest lasted four days and in the end the jury returned a verdict of suicide.

Heartbroken, Jeremy and Rachael resolved to continue their fight for justice for their father. It was too late to see him released from prison but now it was their goal to successfully appeal against his conviction and clear his name posthumously.

Shortly after Park's conviction, Jeremy and Rachael asked

well-known investigative journalist Bob Woffinden, who specialised in miscarriages of justice, to write about their father. In a piece for the *Daily Mail* published two days after Park's suicide, Woffinden wrote, "I went to meet Jenny and Jeremy – Rachael lives in China – and I came away impressed with their commitment. Jeremy had already put together a thorough document exposing what he says are the flaws in the evidence and analysing all the circumstances surrounding the case."

Woffinden was working on a book about cases he termed 'casualties of justice'. He had in mind a book similar to *No Smoke!* by Sandra Lean, and agreed to write a chapter on Gordon Park. Published in 2016, the book would be called *The Nicholas Cases*. It took its name from the story of St Nicholas of Myra, the fourth century Greek Christian bishop, who was known for his compassion and became the patron saint of travellers. He was also enshrined in our culture as Santa Claus.

It was a lesser known story, however, that Woffinden drew on for his title in which St Nicholas halted the execution of three young men wrongly convicted of a crime.

He had already written extensively in newspapers about Park's claim to be innocent and the spurious basis for his conviction. In a lengthy piece for the *Daily Mail* he examined the evidence that put Park behind bars and tested its validity, claiming the jury's verdict had been unsafe.

The book's blurb read, "Here are the private stories of ten people who have all been found guilty of serious offences. They received long prison sentences that have ruined their lives and, all too often, ruined the lives of their families as well. [...] If they were being properly punished for their crimes, then that is as it should be. But were they treated by the trial and appeal processes with competence and fairness? What if there is a mystique about the law that, still today, masks a disturbing reality? These cases all deserve to be causes célèbre."

Woffinden compiled 10 cases that he considered to be miscarriages of justice and Gordon Park's was chapter six: 'The missing missing person's inquiry'.

Woffinden worked closely with Jeremy and Rachael in preparing the chapter, making a series of challenges to the accepted narrative. It is a difficult piece to read, emotionally charged as it puts the reader into the heads and hearts of Park's children. It is a thorough explanation of why they believed their father to be innocent.

In the chapter's conclusion, Woffinden doesn't offer platitudes, instead he lets the poignant words of Jeremy and Rachael hang in the air. They describe how their father, after five years in prison, took his own life out of desperation. Jeremy is quoted as saying his father's death was an act of defiance against a corrupt legal system that had badly let his father down. He believed his father did it to relieve the pressure on his children and Jenny.

"He didn't want us to suffer any more," Jeremy is quoted as saying.

Rachael said, "It's so hard to see someone go through so much pain and be powerless against the system. At the end, I wasn't able to take him in my arms and give him a big hug and say how much I loved him, but he knew, I'm sure he knew. That's the only thing that gives me a tiny bit of peace."

Whether you believe Park was guilty or not, one cannot fail to be affected by the words of his heartbroken children.

37

The Appeal

Gordon Park had been dead for a decade when the coda to the Lady in the Lake story came in 2020. It would be the culmination of his family's protracted legal campaign to appeal against the 2005 murder conviction.

Of course by this time the FreeGordon website had long been redundant: Gordon was no longer around to be freed. Whatever posthumous victory Jeremy or Jenny had imagined could now only ever be symbolic.

In August 2010, seven months after Park's death, Jenny made an application to the Criminal Cases Review Commission, the watchdog for miscarriages of justice. She wanted a review of her husband's case.

There would be a long wait. Eight years, in fact.

The watchdog meticulously re-examined the evidence from the trial and also the police files in order to form a decision. In 2016, the *North West Evening Mail* ran a report that began: 'A probe by 'cold case' investigators into evidence used to convict wife killer Gordon Park is now into its sixth year.'

In an interview with the paper, Ivor Price's daughter Kay was critical of Jeremy and Jenny Park for seeking to appeal against the conviction, "They just seem to keep dragging it on, we all know the truth and I'm sure deep down they know too. It's gone on far too long for the decision to be changed and they need to leave us in peace with our fond memories of Carol."

The case review watchdog's decision came in 2018, and it had indeed found there were four points that might cast doubt on the safety of Park's conviction.

The first was a claim the prosecution counsel at the trial failed to disclose evidence of the drug use of Michael Wainwright, the witness who alleged Park's prison confession. Potentially such evidence at the trial would have undermined the safety of Wainwright's testimony.

The second related to an ice-axe found at Park's home in 2004 and the non-disclosure to jurors that pathologist Dr Tapp did not believe it was the murder weapon.

The third point arose from fresh DNA evidence gathered since Park's conviction: samples derived from the knots on the ropes binding the body were not Gordon Park's, they were from another male.

The final compelling point addressed the disputed rock found in the lake. It was the expert view of a geologist instructed by Park's legal team for the 2008 leave-to-appeal hearing, which subsequently had not been heard in court. This new expert assessment contested the prosecution conclusions at the trial.

It was the view of the watchdog that "the balance of the case [had] shifted to such an extent" that Park's case should be referred to the Court of Appeal (Criminal Division). The appeal process has a deliberate set of hurdles to test the robustness of a conviction. If these hurdles are cleared, an appeal may be allowed. On 26 October 2018, convinced by the watchdog's report, Lady Justice Heather Hallett gave permission for the Park family to proceed with such an appeal. The hearing date was set for the following November.

My *Westmorland Gazette* colleague Mike Addison, the journalist who first wrote about the Lady in the Lake case in 1997, now brought the paper's readers up to date with the latest development. His piece on 26 October 2018 was headlined: 'Gordon Park's Lady in the Lake murder conviction referred to Court of Appeal'.

There had been little media interest in the Lady in the Lake case in the years immediately following Park's suicide but Jeremy Park now found himself back in the spotlight in the winter of 2019. As he and Jenny walked along the Strand in the City of Westminster on Tuesday, 5 November, he must have had a sense of trepidation.

The Court of Appeal (Criminal Division) sits within the Royal Courts of Justice, one of the most famous law courts in the world, surrounded by the four historic Inns of Court: Gray's Inn, Lincoln's Inn, Inner Temple and Middle Temple. It is an intimidating building, constructed in the Victorian Gothic Revival style, took 11 years to be completed and was opened by Queen Victoria in 1882. Two years after the Park appeal, it would be used for Nightingale Court hearings relating to the pandemic.

As appellants, the Parks would be represented at the hearing by Henry Blaxland QC; acting for the Crown Prosecution Service, the respondent to the appeal, was Richard Whittam QC. The appeal was to be heard before Mr Justice Sweeney, President of the Queen's Bench Division, and Mrs Justice May.

The hearing began with a representation by Blaxland who, at the age of 65, was a seasoned barrister of four decades. Notable defendants he had represented included disgraced broadcaster Jonathan King and Waheed Ali, who was cleared of involvement in the 7/7 London Tube bombings in 2005.

Blaxland was a staunch defender of the due process of the law. "It works on the principle that it's better for nine guilty people to go free than for one innocent person to be wrongly convicted," he would tell a reporter the following year in a newspaper profile.

Jeremy and Jenny Park had invested their faith in Henry Blaxland and the law. It was their hope that the one innocent person wrongly convicted would turn out to have been Gordon Park.

Blaxland went into great detail, picking over the main themes of the case put forward by the Crown Prosecution Service at Park's trial in 2005, suggesting flaws in the way evidence had been presented.

He poured cold water on the idea that Park was guilty of murder based on his known interest in sailing and mountaineering and familiarity with Coniston Water. He was also scornful of the suggestion that Park had murdered Carol at home, which did not allow for the logistical problem of three children being present in the house.

Blaxland said a fresh assessment of the rock recovered from Coniston Water by a geologist instructed by Park's legal team destroyed claims at the trial that the stone came from the wall at Bluestones.

But Blaxland was most damning of the prosecution's reliance upon the evidence of Michael Wainwright and the disputed ice axe. Wainwright's credibility as a witness would have been destroyed had his drug use been disclosed to the jury at the trial, Blaxland asserted. Neither had the jury been told that pathologist Dr Tapp had doubts that the ice axe was the murder weapon. In preparation for the appeal, Dr Tapp had been shown the axe by representatives from the CCRC. It had been 15 years since he had last seen it; the previous occasion had been prior to Park's trial. Tapp did not believe this axe could have delivered the injuries that killed Carol as it wasn't wide enough or hefty enough. This view had been supported by two dental experts who reviewed the evidence.

As Blaxland spoke, the axe in question was wrapped in a plastic bag and propped against a seat at the back of the Court of Appeal.

Blaxland concluded by telling the judges, "May I make it plain that it is our submission that, however one looks at it, the material that is now available should lead this court to come to the conclusion that this conviction is not safe.

"This is a case, a circumstantial case, where it is very difficult to tell exactly what it was that influenced the jury in their decision."

Now, Richard Whittam QC stood to address the judges and to present the response of the Crown Prosecution Service. He was an equally distinguished barrister, having prosecuted in the trials following the murders of Fusilier Lee Rigby and MP Jo Cox.

Whittam addressed each of the points raised by Blaxland and concluded that the evidence against Park when considered in its entirety was strong. He said that the matters of non-disclosure from the trial and the new evidence presented by the appellants were not significant enough to affect the safety of the conviction.

The appeal hearing was detailed and taxing, lasting until Wednesday, 7 November. As Jeremy and Jenny walked out of the Royal Courts of Justice on to the Strand, they knew there was another long wait ahead before they would receive the judgement.

The appeal hearing, inevitably, generated headlines. The *Daily Mirror* said: 'Son's bid to clear dead dad of 'Lady in the Lake murder' heard at Court of Appeal.' The BBC reported: '"Lady in the Lake' murder: Gordon Park's conviction 'unsafe".' Barrow's *North West Evening Mail* went with: 'Teacher's conviction for 'Lady in the Lake' murder was 'unsafe', court hears'.

The *Westmorland Gazette* took a slightly different approach: 'Lady in the Lake murder appeal: 'I hope the family get some kind of closure from this'.' *Gazette* reporter Tom Murphy quoted a councillor on South Lakeland District Council, Mark Wilson, who had known Gordon Park when both were teachers in Barrow. Wilson said, "After all these years, I hope the family get some kind of closure from this. Hopefully the new evidence will help solve the case once and for all and the truth is able to come to light."

Of Park, he said, "He seemed to have a reasonable career as a teacher when I knew him. I'm pleased his family have stood by him through everything after all this time."

Listening to the appeal hearing at the Royal Courts of Justice was Doug Marshall. Almost a quarter of a century had passed since the fateful phone call at the Railway pub in Dalton-in-Furness. It had sent him, a young Detective Constable, to the shoreline at Coniston Water. He hadn't known it at the time, but his life had changed at that moment.

In the years since 1997 he had risen through the ranks:

Detective Sergeant, Detective Inspector, Detective Chief Inspector and Detective Superintendent. He had led major national police operations and been Senior Investigating Officer in cold case reviews of undetected crimes in Cumbria.

And yet the Carol Park case kept pulling him back.

It had been two decades since the days of carrying the case file everywhere he went. After all this time he still felt a duty to Ivor Price, a duty to see that justice was done for Carol.

He had believed Park's conviction in 2005 would be the end of it. But each time the Park family sought to appeal, he felt it necessary to personally oversee the police's response.

When I spoke to Marshall for this book in 2023, he chose his words carefully. He didn't want to give the impression that he alone was capable of preparing for the Court of Appeal hearing, but in his view it had made sense that he saw the job through.

"It did rely a lot on previous knowledge," he told me, "and it would have been extremely difficult for anyone else to have picked that up and understand the nuances."

It would have taken months for another officer to read all the evidence and background papers just to get up to speed.

"And we didn't have that time," he said.

The year was 2019. It was 43 years since Carol Park went missing, 22 years since her body was discovered in the lake, 14 years since Gordon Park's conviction, almost a decade since his suicide. Now the fate of Park's posthumous reputation was in the hands of the appeal judges.

If they upheld the appeal, decades of investigative work by Doug Marshall and Cumbria Police would be reduced to ash, in turn denying Ivor Price's family the satisfaction of justice for Carol.

If they rejected the Park family's appeal, Gordon Park would for eternity be known as the man who murdered the Lady in the Lake.

For now, there was nothing either party could do but wait.

Epilogue

News of the 2019 appeal hearing passed me by. It was the first time I had missed a development in the case in more than 20 years.

Circumstances in my life had changed over the years. I left newspapers just before Christmas 2015. Sales of traditional print newspapers had been in decline since the turn of the century, thanks to the advent of the internet which ripped the heart out of their advertising revenue. Once upon a time, if you were looking for a new job or wanted to buy a house or a car, you trawled through your local paper. But now all of that advertising money – and it had been considerable – had migrated online and the big newspaper owners were slow to react.

This body-blow led to journalists being laid off in their droves. I witnessed many of my colleagues being squeezed out of the industry they loved. It signalled a sad decline in the influence of newspapers to hold power to account, one from which legacy news organisations have never truly recovered in my view.

When I was offered voluntary redundancy, I was ready to go. I had worked continuously as a staff journalist for 23 years and it would take a long time to reset my mindset after the relentless grind of deadlines. The next phase in my career began when

I became a lecturer in multimedia journalism at Manchester Metropolitan University early in 2016. Walking on to the university campus was like a rush of blood to the head. Suddenly I could breathe again. During those final years in newspapers I had felt battered. Now I didn't have an editor or advertising manager tapping their watches. No longer did I feel ground down; I felt released.

That's not to say I breezed into my new profession. Learning to teach, to find the confidence to stand in front of a lecture theatre of students was challenging, I'll admit. I found it scary but exhilarating and ultimately the new role gave me the headspace I'd been looking for. Best of all, my university bosses said, "Continue to do your journalism, write a book and bring what you learn into the lecture theatre for the benefit of your students."

And that was the genesis of my first book, *The Jigsaw Murders*. I wanted to attempt a true story told in the style of fiction. I began thinking about a suitable story. I was in some turmoil at the time as Mum had died unexpectedly a few months earlier and we'd moved Dad into a nursing home near us in Cheshire as he couldn't live by himself in Kendal due to his dementia. Visiting each day and watching him slowly withdraw from the world was difficult, but we would see glimpses of his true personality, usually when I played a piece of music he liked. I became reflective and thought much about my childhood. It was a memory of him talking about the 1935 Ruxton murders in Lancaster that started me writing the book.

There are strong parallels between Dr Buck Ruxton's crimes told in *The Jigsaw Murders* and the Lady in the Lake case. Both are stories of a woman killed by her husband; in each case the killer was a proud, controlling man. Each is believed to have committed his crime while his children (three in each man's case) were in the house. There was no design on my part to write books with such parallels, they were simply stories that intrigued me. Once *The Jigsaw Murders* was published, the Lady in the Lake case seemed a natural follow-up.

When I caught up with my reading on Jeremy Park's appeal bid in 2019, I found I had unanswered questions. Why had Park's family fought for so long to clear his name? Why had the case dragged on for so long after Park's 2005 conviction? I knew that a healthy list of questions would be the engine driving a book about the case.

I was intrigued by this family loyalty in the face of such a welter of circumstantial evidence. Since 1997 I had been convinced Gordon Park was guilty. This conviction had only hardened when I saw him at Carol's inquest the following year.

Even allowing for the possibility that Park's cold demeanour might be an idiosyncratic display of grief following the discovery of his wife's body, the more I heard of his defensive behaviour the more I believed he was a cold and calculating killer.

It is true, there had been no 'smoking gun' to convict him. In 1997, DNA evidence to solve cold cases had been used for a decade, but the problem in the Park case was the time that had elapsed since Carol went missing. The trail had truly gone cold.

To my mind, and the jury clearly agreed, the lack of a single, irrefutable piece of evidence was less of a problem when one considered the overwhelming circumstantial evidence. When taken as a whole, you were left with only one candidate as the murderer: Gordon Park.

He had the motive and the opportunity to kill his wife. He

was skilled in tying knots, he knew Coniston Water intimately and had kept a boat on the lake. Then there were the outright lies he told in court that he later tried to explain away as slips of memory when challenged: his claim to have not worn glasses prior to 1976; the sale entry in his boat's logbook coinciding with the month of Carol's disappearance.

I believe Park murdered Carol and then spent two decades keeping his own children in the dark as they pined for their mother while also watching his brother-in-law's heart break at the loss of a second sister. All to save his own skin. That would take a very callous person. That was the sort of man I believed Gordon Park to be.

And so I began work on this book. I set aside my feelings about Park, wanting to examine the story journalistically, including the possibility he had been innocent. I knew a lot of my research would be found in newspaper and television news archives. I would need to consult the public records of the case, too: transcripts of the trial and the appeal hearing, as well as police interviews with Gordon Park.

I drew up a list of people I felt I should speak to, who were essential to the story. I knew I would need to approach members of the Park and Price families, to seek their thoughts.

The first interview I conducted, however, was with the man who had been the glue holding Cumbria Police's investigation together over the years: Doug Marshall.

In March 2023, I clicked into a video call and waited for Doug's face to appear on my laptop. In my initial research, his name kept cropping up. I searched for him on Facebook and discovered we had a mutual friend.

I messaged Chris Bethell, one of my old friends from Queen

Katherine School in Kendal. Chris's mother worked in the circulation department of the *Westmorland Gazette* when I was a young reporter, while Chris briefly sold advertising after school before joining Cumbria Police. It was during his time as a police constable that he became friends with Doug Marshall.

Chris, who would go on to become a detective himself, recalled the dramatic activity at Barrow Police Station in 1997 when Carol Park's body was found. He remembered an awful smell pervading the corridors when the clothing evidence from the body was brought into an interview room. He recalled meeting Gordon Park in the custody office prior to being interviewed by detectives.

Chris put me in touch with Doug.

Now, thanks to patchy Wi-Fi, which occasionally caused Doug's face to pixelate, we were able to talk. At the time, he was still a Senior Investigating Officer at Cumbria Police. Running parallel to this, he was two years into a five-year spell as the Judicial Appointments and Conduct Ombudsman, overseeing complaints relating to judges and magistrates. He is also the director of Hawk Detective Services, based in Scotland, where he uses his expertise in managing undercover operations and in the field of witness protection.

I interviewed Doug for more than five hours across two interviews and he described the events of the previous 25 years, from the night he was playing pool at the Railway pub in Dalton to the appeal hearing in London in 2019.

I wanted to know why, in all that time, he had never given up.

It was simple, he explained. He had felt a weight of responsibility, especially to Ivor Price and his family.

"It's really important to manage people's expectations," he

said. "I couldn't guarantee anything, but I wanted to reassure them that we were still trying."

He continued, "Mr and Mrs Price were such nice people. They never put any pressure on us. I've worked with very demanding families over the years in some cases. It wasn't like that. They were really grateful that people were still trying to get justice for Carol."

I had wanted to speak to Home Office pathologist Dr Edmund Tapp but sadly he had died aged 88 in March 2022, just a few months before I began work on this book. In April 2023, I contacted his son, Nigel Tapp, who is an estate agent living in Cheshire. Nigel said his father had been proud of his achievements and would have been pleased his work was gaining recognition.

"He would talk about his work, his cases," Nigel told me. "He would say: 'I have done a strangler today.'"

He described his father as "an organised hoarder" and when he died Nigel inherited boxes and boxes of his murder files. "Nothing was too small, such as a fax from the police. He was orderly," he said. "I had to make a moral judgement out of respect to the families [of the murder victims] so I didn't keep it all."

I asked whether he had the file from the Carol Park case. He said he would check and let me know. A few days later I got an email from him. He'd not found any files but he had discovered a couple of VHS tapes labelled 'the Lady in the Lake'. He sent them to me and they turned out to be recordings of television documentaries in which Dr Tapp had featured. The tape reminded me of Dr Tapp's warm, northern accent, and he was just as I remembered him at Carol Park's inquest in 1998.

Sadly, Ivor Price, too, had died before I began this book, the consequence of an asbestos-related illness. The coroner at Carol's hearing also presided over Mr Price's inquest.

I interviewed Ian Smith by telephone in December 2023. Once HM Senior Coroner for South and East Cumbria, he is now retired. In 2021, he published his memoirs, called *More Deaths Than One: A Coroner at the turn of the Millennium.* It is a fascinating read, covering the varied and often high-profile inquests he oversaw.

Mr Smith draws out a number of poignant observations with regard to Carol Park's murder. During his research, he came across a *North West Evening Mail* story in which Ivor Price described his sister meeting Donald Campbell in 1955.

Mr Smith writes, "I saw enough of Ivor Price to trust what he said and to know he would not invent something like this for effect. It means that the people in two of my highest profile inquests met and that in each case they were recovered from Coniston and in each case decades elapsed between their death and the finding of the body. I find this remarkable and even a little shocking."

Mr Smith told me what he believed were the circumstances leading to this meeting. Apparently, Campbell was good friends with Conservative politician Edward du Cann. At the 1955 General Election, du Cann stood unsuccessfully as the Tory candidate for Barrow-in-Furness and it is likely that Campbell was helping him to campaign in the shipbuilding town. It was probably during house-to-house visits that the encounter between nine-year-old Carol and Campbell occurred.

In the acknowledgements to his memoir, Mr Smith thanks Dick Binstead, the Crown Prosecution Service solicitor, for sharing advice about writing and publishing. Binstead had published an account of the Carol Park case, based on his own case files and the same court transcripts I was now consulting. *A Very Cumbrian Murder: The Tragic Story of the Lady in the Lake* appeared in 2016 under his full name, Douglas Richard Binstead, covering the story prior to the Parks' appeal.

In an interview with the Carlisle *News and Star* when his book was published, Mr Binstead explained his motivation. For years he had considered writing a book as the case had fascinated him but it was reading Sandra Lean's book *No Smoke!* that finally spurred him into action. He felt he had to write a book to counter her criticism of the way Gordon Park's case was dealt with by the criminal justice system.

In his memoir, Mr Binstead said he had been convinced of Park's guilt since the very first investigation in 1997. "There is only one candidate on the shortlist," he wrote, "and there has never been another. The guilt of Gordon Park shines out like a beacon."

Mr Binstead might have been incensed by Sandra Lean's book, but when his memoir came out it upset Ivor Price's daughter, Kay. In an interview with the *North West Evening Mail* on 21 September 2016, she criticised him for not speaking to her family as part of his research. "I could have told him how the family felt and how awful it was for us having to see Gordon acting all smarmy in court," she told the reporter.

Of her cousins' attempt to clear their father's name, she said, "I can't blame them." She added that any child who loved their father would do the same.

In writing this book I had no desire to pry into the lives of Jeremy Park and his family, nor did I wish to cause distress. But

I knew that if this work was to have journalistic integrity, at some point I would have to make contact. I approached both Jeremy Park and Ivor Price's daughter Kay, but neither wished to be interviewed.

Friday, 1 May 2020.

And so the final revelation in the Lady in the Lake story came to pass.

The UK was in a state of lockdown, the first to be called by Prime Minister Boris Johnson in response to the Covid-19 pandemic. The world was in freefall and the future was uncertain.

Uncertainty was something Jeremy Park and his family had lived with for a decade. Uncertainty hung over their campaign to clear Gordon Park's name. The answer lay within the pages of the judgement that was made public on that sunny Friday.

It was not the news they were hoping for.

The senior judges, led by Mr Justice Sweeney, had considered all the evidence from the case and the representations at the appeal hearing. They had taken six months to consider their judgement. At the end of the complex and detailed 81-page document was a single line: "For the reasons set out above, we have no doubt as to the safety of the conviction. Therefore, the appeal is dismissed."

It was over. Gordon Park's conviction would stand.

A statement from Jeremy and the rest of the Park family was issued to journalists by legal executive Maslen Merchant of Hadgkiss, Hughes and Beale Solicitors.

It read: "The family, friends and supporters of Gordon Park, and Carol Park's children, are disappointed with today's decision. Having exhausted all options, we are now left without the closure we were all hoping for. The judgement marks the end of our fight to clear his name."

Inevitably, the judgement was welcomed by Ivor Price's daughters, Kay and Claire. Through a statement issued by Cumbria Police, they said, "Our auntie Carol had suffered a tragic death and we were relieved that she could now rest in peace and our family could move forward and remember her with the love and dignity she deserved.

"Today is closure for us and we are relieved that this is the last appeal that can be sought and we can now live our lives remembering our auntie as the beautiful auntie she was."

For Doug Marshall, the judgement drew a line under a case that had taken a lifetime to resolve. He had done his duty to the memory of Ivor Price and he had seen that justice had been done for Carol.

January 2024.

The biting wind of the Irish Sea whipped at the collar of my coat. I was in Barrow-in-Furness. I'd come to sift through back copies of the *North West Evening Mail* on microfilm at the town's library. I'd also planned to drive to Leece to see Bluestones and then, if there was time, take the road to Ulverston and then on to Coniston Water, following Doug Marshall's route on that August night in 1997.

I underestimated how long it would take to go through the old newspapers, threading the microfilm onto the wheels of the machine and then scrolling through hundreds of pages in search of stories about the Lady in the Lake.

It was almost 5pm when I finished. I had what I needed. I

rewound the last reel, carefully slid it into its cardboard box and slotted it in correct-date order in the filing cabinet. I thanked the staff and left the library.

The light was thin. It would be dark within 20 minutes. Coniston was a good hour away, so I abandoned that idea. I could still get to Leece.

I walked along Duke Street, the wind trying to lift me off my feet, spots of rain flecking my coat. Gulls wheeled noisily overhead. The Town Hall was straight ahead, where Carol Park's inquest was held.

I got into my car on Market Street and headed out of Barrow. The light was evaporating and by the time I reached Leece it was completely dark. I could see nothing but the lights from cottage windows. It was impossible to find Bluestones. It didn't matter, I had seen it when I visited in 1997. I knew it was a pretty place, but now it felt eerie.

The ice symbol pinged on the dashboard as the road under my wheels took me out of Leece. I passed a gritter truck which sprayed salt across my windshield; to my right I could see a string of lights in the distance like a precious necklace. The lights of Barrow.

It was time to leave Furness, to leave Cumbria; it was time to go home and lay to rest the ghosts of the past.

This is a story of a murder. It is also a story of mothers and fathers, and of children.

Now this story is told.

Acknowledgements

I am indebted to the following people for their kind assistance while I was researching and writing *The Lady in the Lake*.

I have known Chris Bethell since we were at high school together in Kendal. I also worked briefly with him at the *Westmorland Gazette* when he was an ad rep before joining Cumbria police at Barrow. Chris introduced me to Doug Marshall – they remain firm friends almost 30 years after their time in the police.

Doug Marshall was incredibly generous with his time and advice. He shared court documents and the wording of his Chief Constable's commendation, and was open about his feelings and thought processes during the two decades of the Park investigation. He admitted that some of the personal things he told me had never been revealed before, so I'm privileged it was me he opened up to.

Nigel Tapp's assistance was invaluable in helping me to understand the life and achievements of his late father, Dr Edmund Tapp.

Mike Addison, my *Westmorland Gazette* colleague, confirmed my memories of the events of August 1997, including his conversation with the member of the Kendal diving club that found Carol Park's body.

ACKNOWLEDGEMENTS

I would like to thank the staff at the libraries in Kendal and Barrow-in-Furness for helping me research the archives of the *Westmorland Gazette* and *North West Evening Mail*. Special mention should go to Kate Holliday, library development officer, and Kate Honour, library assistant, at Kendal Library, who showed me how to operate the microfilm reader. Kate Holliday gave me a short tour of the building; it brought back memories of when I worked there on weekends while still at school. Kate Holliday invited me to give a talk about *The Jigsaw Murders* at Kendal Library in October 2023, which I was delighted to do.

Steven Ramshay, Communications Manager at Cumbria Constabulary, provided advice on accessing transcripts of detectives' interviews with Gordon Park.

Professor Caroline Wilkinson leads Face Lab, the pioneering facial reconstruction research group at Liverpool John Moores University. Now best known for showing the world what Jesus, St Nicholas and Richard III looked like, she kindly spoke to me about reconstructing Carol Park's face for Dr Tapp in 1997 at the University of Manchester.

Retired coroner Ian Smith was generous in speaking to me in January 2024. He discussed his memories of the Carol Park inquest, as well as other hearings he has presided over. He also sent me the *North West Evening Mail* cutting in which Ivor Price mentioned his sister had met Donald Campbell.

Keith Harrison, the former head teacher of South Newbarns Junior School, shared his few memories of Gordon Park from their time working together.

University of Derby academics Melanie Haughton and Dean Fido kindly explained the psychology behind the appeal of true crime.

I am grateful to Jeremy Park and Kay Washford for responding to my requests for interviews. My messages out of the blue must have been disconcerting. Although each declined to talk, I would like to thank them for doing so graciously.

A huge thank you to my agent Joanna Swainson for her faith in this book (after the two ideas that became lost down blind alleys), and to Chris Brereton, Christine Costello and the team at Mirror Books for all their support. My editor Christine, in particular, made great editorial suggestions that pushed me to produce a tighter, more coherent manuscript.

Love and thanks, as always, to my beautiful family: my wife Louise and our precious children, Emily and Matthew.

APPENDIX

SOURCES

Court documents:

Transcript of trial (T2004/7403), Regina v Gordon Park, before the Honourable Mr Justice McCombe, Wednesday, 26 January 2005, at the Crown Court, the Courts of Justice, Crown Square, Manchester.

Approved judgement in appeal (case number 201804430 B3) between Gordon Park (deceased) and Regina, before Mr Justice Sweeney and Mrs Justice May DBE, at the Royal Courts of Justice, Strand, London, on 1 May 2020.

Archives:

Westmorland Gazette archive, Kendal Library's local studies centre.

North West Evening Mail archive, Barrow Archive Centre, Barrow-in-Furness Library.

The National Archives, Kew.

Newspapers and journals:

Aberdeen Press and Journal

BBC News

Blackpool Gazette

British Medical Journal

Carlisle News and Star

Daily Record

The Guardian

Daily Mail

Daily Telegraph

The Independent

Irish Examiner

Kent Online

Lancashire Telegraph

Lancaster Guardian

Liverpool Echo
Mail on Sunday
Middlesbrough Gazette
New Scientist
North West Evening Mail, Barrow-in-Furness
Northern Echo
Press Association
Press Gazette
The Scotsman
Shropshire Star
Teesside Gazette
Westmorland Gazette
Whitehaven News

Interviews:

Mike Addison, former *Westmorland Gazette* journalist and colleague. Facebook messages with the author: February 2023.

Chris Bethell, friend and former Cumbria Police officer, Facebook messages with the author: February 2023.

Jennie Dennett, former *Westmorland Gazette* reporter. Emails with the author, 4 January 2023.

Keith Harrison, former head teacher of South Newbarns Junior School: telephone interview, 10 March 2023.

Sandra Lean, author of *No Smoke! The Shocking Truth About British Justice.* Facebook correspondence with the author: December 2023

Doug Marshall: video interviews, 3 March and 17 March 2023.

Steven Ramshay, communications manager, Cumbria Constabulary: video interview, 25 April 2023.

Ian Smith, HM Senior Coroner for South and East Cumbria, retired: telephone interview, 20 December 2023.

Nigel Tapp (son of the late Dr Edmund Tapp): initial Facebook discussion; subsequent interview: 27 April 2023.

Kay Washford (nee Price, Ivor Price's daughter): Email correspondence March 2023; subsequent telephone conversations: 30 March and 3 April 2023.

Professor Caroline Wilkinson of Liverpool John Moores University, expert in facial reconstruction and director of the groundbreaking Face Lab, a research group conducting forensic and archaeological research and consultancy work. Email communication: 11 May 2023. Telephone interview: 12 May 2023.

Books:

Binstead, Douglas Richard. *A Very Cumbrian Murder: The Tragic Story of the Lady in the Lake.* Peterborough: FastPrint Publishing, 2016.

Burn, Gordon. *Somebody's Husband, Somebody's Son: The Story of the Yorkshire Ripper.* London: Pan, 1985.

Chandler, Raymond. The Lady in the Lake and other novels. London: Penguin, 2001

Capote, Truman. *In Cold Blood.* London: Penguin, 1967.

David, A. Rosalie (ed). *Manchester Museum Mummy Project: Multidisciplinary Research on Ancient Egyptian Mummified Remains.* Manchester University Press, 1979.

David, Rosalie & Tapp, Eddie (eds). *Evidence Embalmed – Modern Medicine and the Mummies of Ancient Egypt.* Manchester: University Press, 1984.

David, Rosalie & Tapp, Eddie (eds). *The Mummy's Tale: The Scientific and Medical Investigation of Natsef-Amun, Priest in the Temple at Karnak.* New York: St Martin's Press, 1993.

Davies, Hunter. *Wainwright: The Biography.* London: Michael Joseph, 1995.

Davies, Hunter (ed.). *The Wainwright Letters.* London: Frances Lincoln, 2011.

De'Cruze, S., Walklate, S. & Pegg, S.. *Murder.* London: Taylor & Francis, 2013.

De Quincey, Thomas and Morrison, Robert (ed.) *Confessions of an English opium-eater and other writings.* New edn. Oxford: Oxford University Press, 2013.

De Quincey, Thomas. *On murder considered as one of the fine arts: and other writings.* Auckland: Floating Press, 2012.

Lean, Sandra. *No Smoke: The Shocking Truth About British Justice.* County Mayo: CheckPoint Press, 2008.

Orwell, George. 'Decline of the English Murder'. *Essays.* London: Penguin, 1994.

Scott, Walter. *The Lady of the Lake.* Project Gutenberg online, originally published 1883.

Smith, Ian. *More Deaths Than One: A Coroner at the Turn of the Millennium.* Newton Stewart: Hayloft Publishing, 2021.

Stainton, I. & Ewin, R. *Criminal Investigation.* St Albans: Critical Publishing, 2022.

Tapp, Edmund. *Tetracycline in Experimental Pathology.* Doctor of Medicine thesis. University of Liverpool, 1964.

Unknown. *Kendal and District Directory 1965/66.* Denton, Lancs: Ashton & Denton Publishing Co. Ltd, 1965.

Whittington-Egan, Richard. *Murder on File.* Glasgow: Neil Wilson Publishing, 2011.

Williams, Emlyn. *Beyond Belief: The Moors Murderers, the Story of Ian Brady and Myra Hindley.* London: Pan, 1968.

Woffinden, Bob. *The Nicholas Cases: Casualties of Justice.* London: Bojangles Books, 2016.

Television News and Documentaries:

BBC News

Granada News, ITV

ITV News

The Body in the Lake: Countdown to Murder, Channel 5, 25 November 2014.

Real Crime: Lady in the Lake, Granada Television, 16 January 16, 2007.

Online:

Alamy.com

Andrewsgen.com

Atlanticchambers.co.uk/

Archiveshub.jisc.ac.uk

Barrowbc.gov.uk

Churchoflowfurness.org.uk

Cumbria.ac.uk

Ebay.com

Forensic-knots.uk

Forresterssolicitors.co.uk

FreeGordon.org

Google Maps

Historicengland.org.uk

Historyofgeology.fieldsofscience.com

Lakestay.co.uk

Legal500.com

Lincolnhousechambers.com

Lunesdale.org/locations/coniston-bailiffs-wood

Murderpedia.org

Nickthorpe.co.uk

Pure.southwales.ac.uk
RIBC.co.uk
Richardwhittamqc.com
Tardis.fandom.com
TheFreeLibrary.com
Wigglesworth.me.uk
YouTube.com – Andy the Diver
Notes on sources

Part One
Chapter 1:

Bailiff Wood and Coniston Water information: Lunesdale Sub Aqua Club website and YouTube video by Andy the Northern Diver. The divers' memories from: *Westmorland Gazette*, 4 February 2005; Channel 5 TV documentary *The Body in the Lake: Countdown to Murder*; news report on the BBC news website of 28 January 2005; the judge's summing up at Gordon Park's 2005 trial; the 2020 Court of Appeal hearing transcript. Use of lift bags in scuba diving: a YouTube video by Azul Unlimited. Mike Addison's account from an interview with the author in March 2023. Doug Marshall memories from video interviews with the author in March 2023. Details about Dr Edmund Tapp drawn from his obituary in the *British Medical Journal*, 4 November 2022, and author interview with his son, Nigel, on 27 April 2023. Police photographs of evidence examined by Dr Tapp, from TeessideLive on 21 July 2019.

Chapter 2:

Events are from Doug Marshall interviews with the author. Dr Tapp's post-mortem examination: 2005 trial transcript, 2020 appeal judgement and *A Very Cumbrian Murder*. Character information about Dr Tapp: author interview with Nigel Tapp and British Medical Journal obituary published on 4th November 2022. DCI Noel Kelly's interview with Granada News: 17 August, used in *Real Crime: Lady in the Lake* (aired 16 January 16, 2007), accessed via VHS tape belonging to the late Dr Edmund Tapp, provided by his son, Nigel Tapp.

Chapter 3:

Mike Addison's front page story: *Westmorland Gazette*, Friday, 15 August 1997. Peter Hogg murder case: Murderpedia.org and Lakestay.co.uk. Police information: Doug Marshall interviews with author. Chronology of the police investigation checked against newspaper reports, Doug Marshall's interview, *A Very Cumbrian Murder* and *North West Evening Mail*, Monday, 18 August 1997.

Chapter 4:

Terry Clifton murders: *Lancaster Guardian*, 22 June 2015. Also: *Lancashire Telegraph*, 30 January 1997. Remarks by DS Ian Douglas: *The Independent*, Friday, 22 August 1997, *Aberdeen Press and Journal*, Saturday, 23 August 1997, the *Daily Record* (Glasgow), 23 August 1997. Doug Marshall interviews with the author. Ivor Price quoted in the *Independent*, 22 August 1997. Media circus descriptions: the *North West Evening Mail*, 14, 15, 20 and 23 August 1997.

Chapter 5:

The *North West Evening Mail*, 20, 21 and 22 August 1997; *The Guardian*: 22 August 1997. *A Very Cumbrian Murder*.

Chapter 6:

Gordon Park in France: *North West Evening Mail*: 23 August

1997; 2005 trial transcript; *A Very Cumbrian Murder*; Doug Marshall interviews with the author. Jeremy Park reaction: *The Nicholas Cases*. Park interview with *Mail on Sunday*, 18 January 1998. Facial reconstruction: author interview with Professor Caroline Wilkinson, 12 May 2023. Richard Neave information: The *New Scientist* article 'I know that face' from 23 November 23, 2016 and Manchester Medical Collection: Biographical Files at archiveshub.jisc.ac.uk.

Chapter 7:

Gordon Park's arrest: *The Nicholas Cases*. Harry Furzeland details: *A Very Cumbrian Murder*. Police search Park's home: *Aberdeen Press and Journal*, 23 August 1997. Also 'Diana, Dodi together again', ibid. Tara Vallente press officer statement at press conference, 24 August 1997: TV documentary, *The Body in the Lake: Countdown to Murder*.

Part Two
Chapter 8:

Early lives of Gordon and Carol Park and friends and family memories: 2005 trial transcript and 2020 appeal judgement; *The Nicholas Cases*; *A Very Cumbrian Murder*; Ivor Price's description of the meeting between Carol and Donald Campbell: *More Deaths than One*. Matlock Teacher Training College: Andrewsgen.com; Wigglesworth.me.uk. Carol's 21st birthday photo: *Daily Mail*, 4 November 2014.

Chapter 9:

Details of Park and Carol's relationship, wedding and Bluestones: *North West Evening Mail*, 15 January 2005; Ivor Price's views: *Real Crime: Lady in the Lake* documentary; 2005 trial transcript and 2020 appeal judgement; *The Nicholas Cases*. Details of Rampside Church: Churchoflowfurness.org.uk. John Rapson's murder of Christine Price: TheFreeLibrary.com; *The Mirror*, 22 August 1997; *A Very Cumbrian Murder*; *The Nicholas Cases*; the *Westmorland Gazette*, 4 Feb 2005.

Chapter 10:

Charlotte Mason teacher training college: Cumbria.ac.uk. Details of Carol's affairs: 2005 trial transcript, 2020 appeal judgement, *A Very Cumbrian Murder*. Interviews with Kay and Claire Price: *The Body in the Lake: Countdown to Murder* documentary. David Brearley details: *The Nicholas Cases*, 2005 and 2020 court documents, Teesside Live, 21 July 2019; Carol and Brearley's Middesbrough home, 21 Scott Road: Google Maps.

Chapter 11:

Park children's visits to Middlesbrough and custody hearing: *The Nicholas Cases*, 2005 and 2020 court documents. Brearley collecting Carol from Bluestones: *Teesside Gazette*, 21 July 2019.

Chapter 12:

Details of Carol's final months at Bluestones and disappearance: 2005 and 2020 court documents; *A Very Cumbrian Murder*. Police investigation: PC Lawson's testimony: *Real Crime: Lady in the Lake* and *The Body in the Lake: Countdown to Murder* television documentaries. PC Alex Miller's search: 2005 trial transcript; *No Smoke!*. Christmas appeal: *North West Evening Mail*, 20 December 1976; *The Nicholas Cases*. Blackpool and *Doctor Who* exhibition in 1976: *Blackpool Gazette*, 3 January and 4 September 2023; Tardis.fandom.com. Charnock Richard sighting of Carol: 2005 trial transcript; *The Nicholas Cases*; *A Very Cumbrian Murder*.

Part Three
Chapter 13:

Reactions to Carol's disappearance: Ivor and Maureen Price and Anne Walker speaking in *Real Crime: Lady in the Lake*. Death of Diana, Princess of Wales: Ebay listing for *Mail on Sunday*, 31 August 1997. Jimmy McGovern and *The Lakes*: The author's *Westmorland Gazette* articles August 1997 and September 1999. Park's arrest and police interviews: 2005 and 2020 court documents; *The Nicholas Cases*; *Real Crime: Lady in the Lake*; author interviews with Doug Marshall; *A Very Cumbrian Murder*, *The Scotsman*, 22 August 1997; *Aberdeen Press and Journal*, 25 August 1997; Press Association photographs of Ivor Price in 1997, sourced at Alamy.com; *Daily Mirror*, 24 November 2014; Details of Park at South Newbarns Junior School: author's interview with former head teacher Keith Harrison. Park's retirement: *North West Evening Mail*, 25 August 1997; *The Nicholas Cases*.

Chapter 14:

Police interviews: The author's interviews with Doug Marshall; television documentary: *Real Crime: The Lady in the Lake*. Park's first court appearance: *Liverpool Echo*, 26 August 1997, *North West Evening Mail*, 26 August 1997. Mike Graham details: Forresterssolicitors.co.uk. Deborah Kermode's report of the hearing: *Westmorland Gazette*, 29, August 1997. DS Douglas's rallying cry: *A Very Cumbrian Murder*. The days after Park's arrest: *North West Evening Mail*, 23 and 25 August 1997. Cumbria Police interview Park children: *The Nicholas Cases*.

Chapter 15:

Westmorland Gazette, 5 and 12 September 1997. Author's photograph of 30th birthday in *Gazette* newsroom, Kendal.

Chapter 16:

Forensic experts and CPS doubts: 2005 and 2020 court documents; *North West Evening Mail*, 9 September 1997; *A Very Cumbrian Murder* and interview with Dick Binstead, Carlisle *News and Star*, 22 September 2016. Rodger Ide on Shipman suicide: *Manchester Evening News*, 3 October 2007. The *Herald*, 22 October 2014. Park on remand and bail: 2005 trail transcript; *The Nicholas Cases; A Very Cumbrian Murder.*

Chapter 17:

CPS drop murder charge: 2005 and 2020 court documents; *The Nicholas Cases*; *A Very Cumbrian Murder*. Reaction: *North West Evening Mail*, 7 January 1998. Roa Island Boating Club history: RIBC.co.uk. Detectives given six months: author's interview with Doug Marshall.

Chapter 18:

Statement by Park's solicitors and subsequent interview with *Mail on Sunday*, 18 January 1998; *North West Evening Mail*, 21 January 2005; *The Nicholas Cases*. Police reaction to interview: Doug Marshall interview with the author.

Chapter 19:

Inquest hearing and Park's arrival: author's news report in *Westmorland Gazette*, 11 September 1998; *North West Evening Mail*, 7, 8 September 1998; *More Deaths than One*. Barrow Town Hall history: Barrowbc.gov.uk; historicengland.org.uk. *Westmorland Gazette* editor Mike Glover: *Press Gazette*, 22 August 2012.

Chapter 20:

North West Evening Mail, 9 September 1998.

Chapter 21:

Doug Marshall's persistence and prison confession evidence: author's interviews with Marshall; 2005 and 2020 court documents; *A Very Cumbrian Murder*; Shafilea Ahmed inquest, BBC News, 11 January 2008.

Chapter 22:

New forensic evidence: 2005 and 2020 court documents; author interviews with Doug Marshall; forensic-knots.uk; *North West Evening Mail*, 11 August 1999 and 14 January 2004; *A Very Cumbrian Murder*. Duncan Pirrie details: pure.southwales.ac.uk. Churchman and Huddleston quotes: *Real Crime: Lady in the Lake*.

Chapter 23:

Park's rearrest and questioning: *North West Evening Mail*, 14 and 15 January 2004, 8 January 2005; author interviews with Doug Marshall; Real Crimes: Lady in the Lake; *A Very Cumbrian Murder*. Park children's reaction: *The Nicholas Cases*.

Chapter 24:

Court appearances: *North West Evening Mail*, 15 and 16 January 2004; *Irish Examiner*, 15 January 2004. Youngs come forward: 2005 trial transcript; Real Crime: The Lady in the Lake; *A Very Cumbrian Murder*. Furness and District Magistrates Court: Google Maps; author visit to Barrow on 12 January 2024. Photo of Park leaving court: PA picture on Alamy by Owen Humphreys.

Chapter 25:

Start of Park's 2005 trial: *The Guardian*, 26 November 2004; the *Northern Echo*, 26 November 2004; the Independent, 26 November 2004; *Yachting Monthly*, 26 November 2004; *North West Evening Mail*, 11 January 2005; PA images via alamy.com; *The Nicholas Cases*; *A Very Cumbrian Murder*. Pastor George Harrison details: *The Nicholas Cases*. Alistair Webster details: Lincoln House Chambers website; *Lancashire Telegraph*, 7 October 1996. Katherine Blackwell details: Lincoln House Chambers website. Andrew Edis details: Atlantic Chambers website.

Chapter 26:

Pirrie evidence: 2005 and 2020 court documents; *Whitehaven News*, 9 December 2004; Historyofgeology.fieldsofscience.com; Doug Marshall interviews with author. Brearley testimony: 2005 and 2020 court documents; *North West Evening Mail*, 5 and 10 January 2005.

Chapter 27:

Trial and jury's visit to Cumbria: 2005 and 2020 court documents; *Westmorland Gazette*, 21 January and 4 February 2005; *North West Evening Mail*, 5, 10, 11, 13, 14, 15, 17 January 2005; *Whitehaven News*, 13 January 2005; *Daily Mail*, 11 January 2005; *Middlesbrough Gazette*, 12 January 2005;

Chapter 28:

Trial evidence: 2005 and 2020 court documents; *North West Evening Mail*, 21, 22, 24, 25, 27, 28 January 2005.

Chapter 29:

Park courts the media before verdict: *Westmorland Gazette*, 4 February 2005; *North West Evening Mail*, 29 January 2005; author interviews with Doug Marshall. Verdict and reactions and Park solicitors' statement: 2005 and 2020 court documents; *North*

West Evening Mail, 28 and 29 January 2005; Doug Marshall interviews with author; *Real Crime: Lady in the Lake*; PA images of Ivor Price, alamy.com.

Chapter 30:

Park writes to *Westmorland Gazette*: author emails with Jennie Dennett, 4 January 2024; *Westmorland Gazette*, 4 February and 4 November 2005.

Chapter 31:

Visits to Park in prison: The Nicholas Cases; Campaign website: FreeGordon.org. Jeremy Park's 2006 interview with *Granada Reports* journalist Matt O'Donoghue, sourced at ITV.com news report from 5 November 2019. Tony Benn support: *Whitehaven News*, 29 March 2007. Pastor George Harrison and vigils: *North West Evening Mail*, 7 October 2008; *Manchester Evening News*, 17 April 2010. Park requests Shipman suicide report: *Daily Mail*, 19 March 2013; ITV News 19 March 2013; BBC News, 19 March 2013. Appeal bid: North West Evening News, 6 December 2007 and 27 November 2008; BBC News 6 December 2007; Carlisle *News and Star*, 7 and 8 December 2007; author interviews with Doug Marshall; *The Nicholas Cases*. Clarion Solicitors: Companies House. Jeremy Park's support of father: *Sunday Herald*, 23 July 2006, sourced at Nick Thorpe's website, nickthorpe.co.uk.

Chapter 32:

Park in prison, suicide and reaction: BBC News, 25 January 2010; *Daily Mail*, 27 January 2010; the Guardian, 29 January 2010; *The Nicholas Cases*. Inquest: BBC News, 19 March 2013; ITV News, 19 March 2013. Woffinden and Park children convinced of Park's innocence: *Westmorland Gazette*, 21 October 2005.

Chapter 33:

Evidence still being investigated: BBC News, 5 November 2019; *Manchester Evening News*, 1 May 2020; *North West Evening Mail*, 4 February 2016. Peter Sutcliffe/Arnside controversy: *North West Evening Mail*, 20 January 2005; the Guardian, 21 January 2005.

Chapter 34:

Appeal bid and review of Park's case: 2020 appeal judgement document; *Daily Mirror*, 8 November 2014; *North West Evening Mail*, 4 February 2016; Press Association, 5 November 2019; *Daily Mirror*, 5 November 2019; ITV News: 26 November 2014 and 5 November 2019; BBC News, 5 November 2019; *Westmorland Gazette*, 26 October 2018 and 7 November 2019; Doug Marshall interviews with author. Royal Courts of Justice history: historicengland.org.uk. Blaxland detail: Kent Online, 22 August 2020. Whittam detail: richardwhittamqc.com; Legal500.com.

Chapter 35:

True crime: author interviews with Melanie Haughton and Dean Fido, of the University of Derby, August 2023. Writing the book: author interviews with Doug Marshall; Dick Binstead criticising Sandra Lean's book: Carlisle *News and Star*, 22 September 2016. John Rapson file at National Archives, Kew: ASSI: 52/1927 – Murder: Rapson, John Paul. Freedom of information outcome: 30 January 2024. Kay Washford criticising Binstead book: *North West Evening Mail*, 21 September 2016. Kay Washford correspondence and phone conversation with